Prisms of Faith

Prisms of Faith

Perspectives on Religious Education and
the Cultivation of Catholic Identity

EDITED BY
Robert E. Alvis
AND
Ryan LaMothe

◐PICKWICK *Publications* • Eugene, Oregon

PRISMS OF FAITH
Perspectives on Religious Education and the Cultivation of Catholic Identity

Copyright © 2016 Wipf and Stock Publishers. All rights reserved. Except for brief quotations in critical publications or reviews, no part of this book may be reproduced in any manner without prior written permission from the publisher. Write: Permissions. Wipf and Stock Publishers, 199 W. 8th Ave., Suite 3, Eugene, OR 97401.

Pickwick Publications
An Imprint of Wipf and Stock Publishers
199 W. 8th Ave., Suite 3
Eugene, OR 97401

www.wipfandstock.com

ISBN 13: 978-1-4982-2990-6

Cataloguing-in-Publication Data

    Prisms of faith : perspectives on religious education and the cultivation of Catholic identity / edited by Robert E. Alvis and Ryan LaMothe.

    x + 152 p. ; 23 cm. Includes bibliographical references.

    ISBN 13: 978-1-4982-2990-6

    1. Identity (Philosophical concept)—Religious aspects—Catholic Church. 2. Christian education. I. Title.

BX926 P75 2015

Manufactured in the U.S.A.   12/14/2015

A Festschrift in Honor of Professor Tom Walters

"Whatever I have learned in my life is questions, and whatever I have tried to share with friends is questions."

—Elie Wiesel

Contents

List of Contributors | ix

Introduction | 1
—*Ryan LaMothe*

1 Use of the Apostolic Fathers in the *Catechism of the Catholic Church* | 10
—*Clayton N. Jefford*

2 "The Mystery Meaning You": Augustine's Mystagogical Preaching on the Church as the Body of Christ | 33
—*Kimberly F. Baker*

3 Catholic Identity and Religious Education in Modern Poland | 52
—*Robert E. Alvis*

4 Christian Education: Rights and Obligations in Light of the 1983 Code of Canon Law | 73
—*Fr. Patrick Cooney, OSB*

5 Liturgical Catechesis and Catholic Identity | 90
—*Diana Dudoit Raiche*

6 Catholic Identity and Adult Moral Formation | 113
—*Fr. Mark O'Keefe, OSB*

7 Religious Education that Promotes Catholic Identity: A Review and Assessment of Approaches | 132
—*Michael P. Horan*

Contributors

Robert E. Alvis earned his PhD in church history from the University of Chicago. Currently he serves as associate professor of church history and academic dean at Saint Meinrad Seminary and School of Theology. His publications include *Religion and the Rise of Nationalism: A Profile of an East-Central European City* (2005) and *White Eagle, Black Madonna: One Thousand Years of the Polish Catholic Tradition* (2016).

Kimberly F. Baker is assistant professor of church history at Saint Meinrad Seminary and School of Theology. She earned her PhD from the University of Notre Dame in 2008 following the defense of her dissertation, "Augustine on Action, Contemplation, and Their Meeting Point in Christ." Her current book project is tentatively titled *Journey to God, Living in Christ: Augustine on the Sacramentality of the Present Life*.

Fr. Patrick Cooney, OSB, JCL, is a Benedictine monk of Saint Meinrad Archabbey. He presently serves as assistant professor of canon law at Saint Meinrad Seminary and School of Theology. In addition to his teaching, Fr. Patrick is a defender of the bond for both the Metropolitan Tribunal in Indianapolis, Indiana, and the Diocesan Tribunal in Evansville, Indiana.

Michael P. Horan is professor of religious education and pastoral theology at Loyola Marymount University, Los Angeles, where he currently serves as associate dean of the College of Liberal Arts. He holds a PhD in religious education from The Catholic University of America. He is the author of two works on the *General Directory for Catechesis* and has published many articles and book chapters on lay pastoral ministry and religious education.

Clayton N. Jefford is professor of Scripture at Saint Meinrad Seminary and School of Theology, where he has taught since 1989. He received his PhD from The Claremont Graduate School in 1988. He has authored or edited eleven published volumes and almost fifty journal articles, primarily related to Scripture and/or the Apostolic Fathers. His most recent publications include the second edition of his *The Apostolic Fathers: A Student's Introduction* (2012), *The Epistle to Diognetus (with the Fragment of Quadratus)* (2013), and *Didache: The Teaching of the Twelve Apostles* (2013). He currently is preparing a commentary on the Didache for publication in the Yale Anchor Bible series.

Ryan LaMothe is professor of pastoral care and counseling at Saint Meinrad Seminary and School of Theology. He earned his PhD from Vanderbilt University in 1994. He has authored four books and over 120 journal articles in the areas of psychoanalysis, pastoral theology, and pastoral counseling. His most recent work is *Missing Us: Re-Visioning Psychoanalysis from the Perspective of Community*. Currently he is writing a book tentatively titled *Care of Souls, Care of Polis: Toward a Political Pastoral Theology*.

Fr. Mark O'Keefe, OSB, holds a doctorate in moral theology from The Catholic University of America and is associate professor of moral theology at Saint Meinrad Seminary and School of Theology, where he has held the posts of president-rector, academic dean, and associate academic dean. His books include *What Are They Saying About Social Sin?* (1990), *Becoming Good, Becoming Holy: On the Relationship of Christian Ethics and Spirituality* (1995), *Deciding to Be Christian: A Daily Commitment* (2012), and *Love Awakened by Love: The Liberating Ascent of Saint John of the Cross* (2014).

Diana Dudoit Raiche holds a PhD from The Catholic University of America. She currently serves as assistant professor in the School of Ministry at the University of Dallas. She has served as a team member with the North American Forum on the Catechumenate, executive director of the religious education department at the National Catholic Educational Association, and as a consultant to the Bishops' Committee on Evangelization and Catechesis.

Introduction

—Ryan LaMothe

WHEN I OPEN A book for the first time, I turn to the dedication page. I am curious about the person the author loves and admires enough to give him/her the first page, the first word, the very introduction to the author's labors. And yet, there is, more often than not, more information on a tombstone than the reader obtains from a single name and a few adjectives. Dedication pages reveal and conceal, teasing our flights of imagination. Who is this person? Why is he important? What role does she play in the life of the author—a muse, a friend, a beloved parent? Happily, for the curious reader and scholar, this introduction includes not only answers to these questions, but also the typical comments regarding the context and content of this book—a *Festschrift* in honor of the life and work of Tom Walters.

A *Festschrift* is an edited book by various contributors who wish to recognize a respected scholar and his/her exceptional contributions to a field of research. This is the case here, but it is also a *liber amicorum*—a book of friends who wish to honor Professor Tom Walters. To honor Tom and to understand his numerous contributions to religious education in the Roman Catholic Church requires going back to his youth and those who influenced him. Tom was born in Detroit, Michigan, prior to the baby boomer generation and during the first month of World War II. It is difficult to say whether growing up in America's Motor City or the city of soul music had much influence on Tom's life, but it is clear that he admired and was shaped by the La Salette Fathers. Indeed, Tom's close identification with these priest-educators was largely the reason for his leaving home after eighth grade to attend the high school seminary they ran in Jefferson City, Missouri. Upon completion of high school and considering priesthood as a life vocation, Tom attended Our Lady of La Salette Seminary in Altamont, New York. His discernment led him to La Salette Major Seminary in Ipswich, Massachusetts, and to taking some courses at Boston College. Before enrolling at The Catholic University of America for a Master of Divinity and after years of discernment, Tom decided that he was not being called to the priesthood and returned home to Michigan.

While Tom realized he was not called to be a priest, his passion for teaching became clearer. It is likely that the La Salette Fathers shaped and nurtured his passion and new vocation. Evidence of this was Tom's desire to teach within the church. Tom began teaching in various Catholic high schools near Detroit during a period of tremendous political unrest and social-cultural changes in the United States. Protests against the Vietnam War, the Civil Rights Movement, race riots in many cities (including Detroit), the assassinations of two Kennedys, Martin Luther King Jr., and Malcolm X, and NASA's moon landing, were some of the events and movements that characterized the turbulent 1960s. Societal and political turmoil accompanied a questioning of the status quo, especially by the baby boom generation. It seems likely that the ferment of this era of questions and change shaped Tom's interest in entertaining and playing with questions. Yet, Tom, born prior to the baby boom generation, also coupled questions and change with a healthy respect for tradition. Indeed, it may have been in the unrest and questioning of the 1960s that Tom learned that one cannot be creative without a respect for—not idolization of—tradition.

During this same period, the Second Vatican Council inspired momentous changes within the Roman Catholic Church. It was a time of *aggiornamento*. The council called for greater lay involvement in the church's life and ministry, which would have a lasting influence on Tom's interest in religion and specifically his concern for and questions about religious education. Tom's passion for religious education eventually led him to enroll in the Pius XII Catechetical Institute at the University of Detroit. At Pius XII, Tom met his future wife, Rita Tyson, who would be an integral partner in and contributor to his professional life, as well as the mother of their three children – Daniel, Rebecca, and David.

Moving away from high school teaching, Tom joined the parish staff of St. Timothy Parish in Trenton, Michigan. As a Director of Religious

Education (DRE), Tom collaborated with Fr. Brian Haggerty on the writing of two sacramental textbooks, one on confirmation, *We Receive the Spirit of Jesus* (1978), and the other on baptism, *We Share New Life* (1979). During the same period, Tom began writing articles in the area of religious education for various Catholic journals. In these early articles, Tom's concerns for accountability in parish catechetical programming and the professionalization of ministry were apparent, as well as his questions regarding effective religious education, all of which would serve as a foundation for the next four decades of his work.

Others took notice of Tom's contributions to the parish and the field. In 1978, Tom was invited to join the Religious Education Office of the Archdiocese of Detroit as supervisor of evaluations. One of his main responsibilities was to assist the archdiocese in finding answers to questions such as: Are parish programs making a difference in participants' lives? What criteria are or should be used to judge effectiveness? Are parishes being realistic in their expectations for religious education programming? These questions reflected the disquiet regarding the archdiocese's catechetical endeavors and its effectiveness in educating children and adults. Tom's leadership, in these efforts, led to his editing the *Handbook for Evaluators*, a compendium of assessment tools for evaluating parish religious education programs. Also during this time, Tom conducted the first of many national surveys profiling the role of the religious education director/catechetical leader.

Tom's questions and his thirst for learning and research led him to the doctoral program in educational psychology at Wayne State University in Detroit. Wayne State was part of the arc of Tom's vocation as an educator. His doctoral education served as an opportunity to continue to deepen and expand his knowledge, hone his research skills, and, more importantly, it enabled him to frame old questions in new ways. The doctorate in educational psychology widened his horizons and opportunities.

After five years of working in the Religious Education Office, Tom applied for a faculty position in religious education at Saint Meinrad Seminary and School of Theology. In the summer of 1983, Tom, Rita, and the kids left the Great Lakes State to settle amid the rolling hills of picturesque southern Indiana. At Saint Meinrad, Tom found a place where he could live out his passion for teaching and research, but not quite as he initially envisioned. After only three years of teaching, school administrators, recognizing Tom's leadership skills, asked him to serve as dean. Because he is a humble and generous person, Tom accepted the position, not realizing at the time that he would end up serving three different terms for a total of seventeen years. The work of a dean is demanding job, especially when one considers that leading faculty members is like herding cats—only more difficult. Yet, Tom's affable nature, good humor, and collegial approach made him an ideal choice for dean, especially during times of transition. Despite the amount of time and energy this new position demanded, Tom continued to be very productive in his research, aided by Rita who collaborated in publishing articles and co-authoring numerous other works. Over the course of his career, he has given over 200 presentations, authored or co-authored 10 book chapters, 21 books, over 60 articles, and 10 book reviews.

To focus on Tom's leadership abilities and scholarly contributions to the field of religious education would overlook another key part of who he is and his contributions to the Catholic Church. For three decades, Tom taught lay and priesthood students. At the heart of his pedagogy is the importance of questions, raising and playing with them and not prematurely arriving at answers. Some of the key questions have been: What is the nature and scope of the profession of catechetical leader? Are catechetical leaders effective in what they claim to be able to do? How do we/they know? What can be expected realistically from the prevalent structure for parish religious education? What does the Catholic community actually look like and how is it informing the church's catechetical efforts? How does the church's emphasis on faith as a gift impact the intended goals and outcomes of catechetical programming and programmatic assessment? Tom's ardor for questions was not simply a teaching method that aimed to enliven the intellectual life of students. It demonstrated for students a way of passing on a religious tradition and faith that are vibrant and dynamic. In other words, Tom's ability to play with questions, to be curious, modeled a type of religious education that is rooted in both *aggiornamento* and tradition. Openness to questions, in short, is part of the passionate creativity that, for Tom, is inextricably anchored in intellectual rigor, imagination, and knowing the tradition. Students, he believes, must ground their catechetical questions and work in sound philosophy and psychology of education, as well as the values and beliefs of the Catholic tradition. For Tom, engaging questions vis-à-vis religious education must accompany a vision—rooted in tradition—that is informed by four essential variables in teaching: teacher, learner, subject matter, and context.

After three decades serving as dean and professor of religious education, Tom retired from teaching, though not from research, which he and

Rita continue to do. In recognition of his contributions to Saint Meinrad Seminary and School of Theology, the church, and his discipline, Tom was awarded the status of professor emeritus. Tom, the modest man that he is, would simply acknowledge this honor with a quick embarrassed nod and word of thanks, leaving the audience and readers unaware of the depth and breadth of his contributions to the field of religious education. To gain an appreciation for Tom's work, one need review his awards:

- 1980 Award of Excellence from *Modern Liturgy* for the baptismal program, *We Share New Life* (Paulist Press, 1979).
- 1981 Sam Gamgee Award for Surprising Service to Religious Education through Research from the Religious Education Association (for doctoral dissertation).
- 2000 National Conference for Catechetical Leadership Research Award for contributions over the years to research in the field of catechetical ministry.
- 2007 Called and Gifted Award from the Association of Graduate Programs in Ministry "in recognition of outstanding leadership and contribution to Graduate Ministry Education."
- 2009 F. Sadlier Dinger Award "in Recognition of Wisdom, Vision and Leadership Serving and Enriching the Ministry of Catechesis."
- 2012 C. Albert Koob Merit Award, received jointly by Tom and his wife, Rita, from the National Catholic Educational Association for "significant contribution to Catholic education . . . [which is] recognized as having current significance at the national level."

These awards are public acknowledgements of Tom's contributions to religious education in the Catholic Church. The La Salette Fathers who influenced Tom would take pleasure in knowing that one of their students would end up doing so much for religious education in the Catholic Church.

Just prior to Tom's retirement from teaching, Dr. Robert Alvis, the dean who took over from Tom in 2010, solicited Tom's colleagues regarding an appropriate retirement gift. What gift would be adequate given Tom's innumerable contributions to Saint Meinrad Seminary and School of Theology and the church? I proffered the idea of a *Festschrift* in honor of Tom's life and work, which Robert quickly organized and led, asking if I would serve as a co-editor. There were enthusiastic responses to this idea by Tom's colleagues at Saint Meinrad and from colleagues in his field to contribute to this book, this *liber amicorum* on religious education. We want to thank each of them for their contributions to this collection. I also would like to acknowledge and thank Robert for his careful editorial eye and his leadership in shepherding this project. Together, we also wish to thank the editors at Wipf & Stock for agreeing to publish this *Festschrift*.

This book falls into two parts. The first set of chapters is more historical in nature, with studies ranging from the early church to the modern period. The second section of the volume has a more contemporary focus, approaching current initiatives and challenges in the formation of faithful Catholics. While each chapter can be read alone, taken together these seven chapters form a coherent whole, illustrating well the perennial importance of Catholic religious education, the various resources and methods employed in this work, and the quotidian challenges that effective formation entails.

The opening chapter is by Clayton Jefford, who examines the use of the Apostolic Fathers in the *Catechism of the Catholic Church* and highlights the strengths, limitations, and future editorial and educational possibilities of using the Apostolic Fathers. Jefford in particular notes that the editors of the *Catechism* rely principally on conciliar authority, Scripture, and patristic literature as three pillars upholding the confessional grounding of religious education. Often overlooked within the last pillar, however, is the use of the writings of the Apostolic Fathers, which Jefford reviews as a distinctive element that enriches ecclesiastical teaching.

Kimberly Baker takes up Augustine's doctrine of the *totus Christus*—the whole Christ with Christ as head and the church as body—as it pertains to his preaching, which was aimed at teaching and forming Christians in their identity in Christ. In this second chapter, Baker considers Augustine's preaching as mystagogical catechesis or instruction that joins Christ, sacrament, and church into one life of love. Love or *caritas*, made manifest by individual Christians and the church, is the sign of identity in Christ. Baker argues that Augustine's preaching on the doctrine of Christ in the context of the liturgy contains important catechetical truths for Catholics today. Namely, it portrays the sacramental reality of the church as the Body of Christ and heightens the sacramental awareness of Christians so that they experience Christ more clearly in the ecclesia's *caritas* and in an individual discipline's acts of love within the church and toward the world.

In chapter three Robert Alvis notes how the complexity of modern life ushered in the necessity of formal education of all citizens. Whereby earlier societies could simply educate the elite, a modern society's survival and flourishing depend on an educated citizenry. This emerging necessity and eventual right often raised political questions about the role of religious education. Recognizing the importance of education in shaping values and virtues, the Catholic Church, with varying success from country to country, sought to participate in this endeavor, though encountering limitations imposed by governments, as well as competing religious and secular worldviews. Alvis examines the church's attempts to defend its rights vis-à-vis education in modern Poland. More particularly, Alvis critically explores four periods of Poland's history and the church's successes and failures in defining formal education. Alvis observes that when the church worked closely with the government in putting its stamp on education, its ability to form young people in the Catholic faith and identity had mixed results. By contrast, when facing hostile governments that restricted Catholic education, Catholics tended to rally around the church, constructing creative opportunities for Catholic education. Alvis's chapter is a cautionary tale in how the church needs to attend to the signs of the times as it pursues the proper formation of the faithful.

The second section of the book contains chapters that address more contemporary features of religious education. In chapter four Fr. Patrick Cooney, OSB, delves primarily into canon law, supported by Second Vatican Council documents, to explicate the rights and obligations of various constituencies within the church with regard to Christian education. He begins by pointing out that the Second Vatican Council's documents agree with modern public documents that proclaim that all persons have an inalienable right to education. The corollary is that all Christians have a right to a Christian education—an inalienable right rooted in baptism. In establishing a right, the next question is what parties are responsible for ensuring that the right to a Christian education is realized. Fr. Cooney, drawing both on canon law and church documents, outlines the various responsibilities of parents, priests, bishops, and the larger community of faith in making the right to a Christian education a reality in the church and society.

In chapter five we move from canon law to liturgy and its role in catechesis and, more particularly, the formation of Catholic identity. Diana Dudoit Raiche sets the context by pointing to several sociological studies that indicate the decline of church attendance, which raises concerns about Catholic identity in the United States. There are, of course, many ways to address concerns about Catholic identity and Raiche focuses her concern on the liturgy as a central formative or catechetical act in the lives of Catholics.

More particularly, she contends that Catholic identity is founded on Jesus's real presence in the Eucharist and the Mass with its symbols, images, prayers, ritual movements, and gestures. Liturgy provides a blend of inductive and deductive catechesis that both forms and sustains Catholic identity.

In chapter six Fr. Mark O'Keefe, OSB, begins by pointing to human science research that shows that US Catholics tend to hold moral positions that are contrary to church teaching and eschew the moral authority of the church in favor of their own personal authority in deciding issues of right and wrong, which suggests that they are being formed by subjectivism. Catholics who regularly attend Mass align themselves more closely with church teaching, but, in light of declining Mass attendance, this offers little cause for celebration. O'Keefe faces these challenging realities head on and asks how the church in the US can shape adult moral formation. He argues that church leaders should consider ways of persuading less committed Catholics to place the value of their Catholic faith at the center of their lives—a re-ordering of values. Because one's values are reinforced by one's participation in a group, this re-ordering is best nurtured by participation in Catholic groups that hold narratives and rituals that form identity and morals. Toward this end, O'Keefe discusses the work of Dean Hoge and his colleagues who offer ten recommendations for enhancing formation, such as attention to the quality of liturgical celebration, promotion of peace and justice, creating hospitable parishes, better adult religious education, and offering formation in spirituality, to name a few. In this era of the new evangelization, O'Keefe also considers the growing prominence of virtue ethics and the promise this approach has in adult formation. While not ignoring the importance of objective moral norms, O'Keefe points out that virtue ethics is primarily concerned not with the question what shall I do, but rather what shall I become? So, a hospitable community and vibrant liturgical celebrations can be key in developing a committed, participative Catholic identity and attending virtues. While O'Keefe notes the many challenges of adult moral formation in the church today, he has confidence and hope in the enduring vitality of Catholic faith.

The concluding chapter is written by Michael Horan. Horan examines three religious education approaches to the formation of Catholic identity in parishes throughout the United States during the past five decades. He begins by identifying and describing these three methods, namely (1) liturgically integrated, (2) shared praxis, and (3) whole community. Using the theological themes of sacramentality, mediation, and communion, which are central to Catholic life and identity, Horan considers each approach in terms of its emphasis. More particularly, he concludes that the liturgically integrated approach accents the theological theme of sacramentality with its focus on the catechumenate and the rich symbolism of Catholic ritual that it communicates. Shared praxis methods highlight the agency of human beings in cooperation with God in seeking and achieving more just communities and societies. A whole community approach stresses the essential importance of the ecclesia with regard to discipleship and communion. Horan ends by suggesting that pastoral leaders, in being aware of the strengths and limitations of each method, engage in critical and constructive conversations about religious education and formation methods and aims.

These authors recognize the importance and complexities of religious education and the ongoing formation of Catholic identity in the twenty-first century. Each, from his/her own discipline, adds rich perspectives that can enliven the necessary conversations that take place in parishes, dioceses, and the larger Catholic Church with regard to forming Catholic identity and fostering discipleship in Jesus Christ. Tom Walters has, for over forty years, been a crucial part of this conversation through his leadership, teaching, research, and scholarly publications. Through this *Festschrift*, this *liber amicorum*, we attempt to recognize and honor Tom's unique voice.

1

Use of the Apostolic Fathers in the *Catechism of the Catholic Church*

—Clayton N. Jefford

Introduction[1]

THE TENDENCY OF WESTERN Christianity to preserve literary records of its tradition has resulted in the formation of catechisms that reflect the elements of confessional faith. The roots of this history likely reside in the ancient desire to preserve some witness of instruction first provided for catechumens at baptism, and in this way these literary records serve as a repository of tradition. Yet we must not think of tradition as simply the recollection of history. As Robert Gnuse observes, it "is a dynamic process, an evolutionary development which grows in response to human religious and social challenges."[2] One might say that a catechism then is a reflection of faith and tradition, yet also a witness to the history of Christian learning that each successive generation of the church experiences. In result, an important task for the editors of each edition of a catechism is to reflect both the witness of historical truth and the response of those who practice it within their culture and society. A catechism is evidence of that process and in result becomes an instrument of education for those who consult it.

---

1. I offer this chapter in honor of Dr. Thomas Walters, a worthy scholar and instructor, but most especially a guiding hand and trusted friend.
2. Gnuse, *No Other Gods*, 290–91.

This is certainly true of the latest edition of the *Catechism of the Catholic Church* (*CCC*),³ which draws its first inspiration from the witness of conciliar tradition, especially derived from the Vatican II Council. At the next step it seeks foundation from Holy Scripture and patristic literature, the latter of which reflects the context within which the parameters of the former were defined. In result, conciliar authority, Scripture, and patristic literature become the primary pillars for what is now offered as the essence of Roman Catholic instruction. These supports subsequently serve as confessional grounding for education within the tradition.

What is often not recognized is the extent to which a fourth cluster of early Christian writings has influenced the *CCC*, that is, the so-called Apostolic Fathers (AF).⁴ Classified by scholars as a subset of works among early patristic literature, these texts were revered but omitted from the New Testament canon.⁵ They include writings attributed to the earliest followers of the apostles, instructions on Christian living, early defenses of the faith, and a martyrology. Their theology was sound; their teachings were widely employed. They served as foundation for much of what evolved into ecclesiastical standards, but their contribution to the tradition often remains misunderstood.

The present essay identifies forty-four usages of the AF within the *CCC* and reflects on how they are employed. In the materials that follow, we offer a quick survey to identify which authors appear within the corpus, an analysis of how each text is used, and a closing summary of conclusions.

---

3. Throughout this essay references are taken from the English translation found in the *Catechism of the Catholic Church* (Collegeville, MN: Liturgical, 1994).

4. Contemporary collections of the AF include *1-2 Clement*, *Shepherd of Hermas*, *Didache*, *Epistle of Barnabas*, Polycarp's *Epistle to the Philippians*, epistles of Ignatius of Antioch (seven considered authentic and five others as spurious), *Martyrdom of Polycarp*, *Epistle to Diognetus*, and fragments of Papias. The *CCC* includes references to five Ignatian epistles, not including those to Polycarp and Philadelphia. Several introductions to the corpus are readily available, see Günther, *Einleitung in die Apostolischen Väter*; Foster, *The Writings of the Apostolic Fathers*; Pratscher, *The Apostolic Fathers*; and Jefford, *Reading the Apostolic Fathers*.

5. Jefford, *Reading the Apostolic Fathers*, 40–54. Athanasius of Alexandria, *Festal Epistle* 39 (dated 367) listed numerous texts later canonized by the church, noting the *Didache* and *Shepherd* as useful for instruction of converts. Other authorities clearly valued such texts, as suggested by the inclusion of *Barnabas* and the *Shepherd* at the end of *Codex Sinaiticus*, as well as *1-2 Clement* in *Codex Alexandrinus*. Their presence in these biblical manuscripts begs for clarification, not to mention Irenaeus' reference to *1 Clement* as "scripture" (*graphē*) in his *Against Heresies* (3.3.3).

Survey of Sources

All authors of the AF are referenced by the editors of the *CCC* with the exception of *2 Clement* and the bishop Papias. Slightly more than forty percent of the references use epistles of Ignatius of Antioch (early second century), with less attention given to the *Didache*, *Diognetus*, and *1 Clement*.

With respect to distribution, references appear as follows: twelve in the first section ("The Profession of Faith"); fourteen in the second ("The Celebration of the Christian Mystery"); fourteen in the third ("Life in Christ"); and four in the final ("Christian Prayer"). Divided according to source, the pattern of usage becomes clear:

AF	CCC I	CCC II	CCC III	CCC IV
Barnabas, Epistle to	0	0	2	0
1 Clement	2	3	1	0
Didache	0	3	2	2
Diognetus, Epistle to	0	0	4	1
Ignatius, Epistles of				
To the Ephesians	1	1	2	1
To the Magnesians	0	1	1	0
To the Romans	3	0	2	0
To the Smyrnaeans	3	1	0	0
To the Trallians	0	3	0	0
Martyrdom of Polycarp	1	0	1	0
Polycarp, *To the Philippians*	0	1	0	0
Shepherd of Hermas				
Visions	1	0	0	0
Mandates	0	0	1	0

One sees the Ignatian epistles evenly employed throughout the first three sections (less so in the fourth) and the *Didache* similarly distributed (though to a lesser extent) among the final three. *1 Clement* is referenced largely in the second section, while *Diognetus* appears mostly in the third. *Barnabas*, the *Shepherd*, the *Martyrdom*, and Polycarp receive the least attention and appear randomly. Prominence is accorded to the epistles of Ignatius, followed by the *Didache* and *1 Clement*, yet less so for *Diognetus*.

Analysis of Usages

In the discussion that follows, the AF are addressed according to appearance within the four divisions of the *CCC*. No significance is attributed to the general distribution itself.

The Profession of Faith

(a) **CCC 496** provides the first use of the AF, citing a creedal fragment from Ignatius in support of Jesus' conception by the Holy Spirit. The text reads:

> You are firmly convinced about our Lord, who is truly of the race of David according to the flesh, Son of God according to the will and power of God, truly born of a virgin, . . . he was truly nailed to a tree for us in his flesh under Pontius Pilate . . . he truly suffered, as he is also truly risen. (*Smyrn.* 1.1–2)[6]

Authority is attributed to Ignatius's words without explanation of his role in the formation of doctrine. This is significant, since much of what he offers is distinctive within extant literature.

Context is deemed irrelevant, though here it is important since the *CCC* seeks to support the virginity of Mary, while Ignatius argues instead for the humanity of Christ.[7] A certain irony ensues to the extent that the bishop challenges docetic opponents at Smyrna, thus requiring him to make a case for Jesus as truly human.[8] This emphasis is not the concern of the editors, however, and is ignored.

---

6. Cited in the notes of the *CCC* in error as *Smyrn.* 1–2, the text is supported in part by Rom 1:1 and John 1:13. All translations of the AF follow those provided in the *CCC*.

7. He argues that Christ was "in the flesh" (*en sarki*) after the resurrection, a conviction drawn from Luke 24:39, though not necessarily shared elsewhere in the New Testament. Thus Matthew says some doubted when they saw him (28:17), and even Luke mentions witnesses who did not recognize him at first (24:13–24), as with Mary Magdalene in the Gospel of John who thought him the gardener and was told not to cling to him (20:11–18). Paul refers to the resurrected body as a "spiritual body" (*soma pneumatikon*; 1 Cor 15:44) with uncertain meaning.

8. Curiously, his observation that Jesus was "united in spirit [*kaiper pneumatikōs*]

The *CCC* thus appeals to an Ignatian creed[9] as support for its position on the virginity of Mary under the assumption that this represents views of the church universal. Offering quick citation of Luke 1:26–27 and Matt 1:23 as accounts for the virginal conception of Jesus,[10] the editors rely on the subsequent authority of Ignatius, having only limited evidence elsewhere.

(b) *CCC* **498** continues its appeal to Ignatius for the principle that "the totality of Christ's mysteries, from his Incarnation to his Passover" is unified. Ignatius proclaims the following:

> Mary's virginity and giving birth, and even the Lord's death escaped the notice of the prince of this world: these three mysteries worthy of proclamation were accomplished in God's silence. (*Eph.* 19.1)[11]

The editors again ignore context, since the bishop continues to explain that such mysteries were soon "revealed to the ages" in the star that the magi followed (Matt 2:1–2, 10). Ignatius's statement here is once more simply accepted without further literary justification. Either the editors are convinced by the bishop's authority or assume his views reflect common teaching. No distinction is made. The issue in question here (i.e., the lack of any comment on the virginal conception in the Gospel of Mark) is identified as a "mystery" by qualification of the bishop's own witness.

(c) *CCC* **760** incorporates a rare usage of the *Shepherd* in which one hears the words "Christians of the first centuries said, 'The world was created for the sake of the Church'" (Herm. *Vis.* 2.4.1). This intriguing reference reflects the author's conviction that the church is eternal in scope, as though a truism of early Christian confession. Similar imagery of the pre-existent church is found elsewhere in *2 Clement* (see 14.1–5),[12] but otherwise is not evident in Scripture or the AF (some scholars argue the author even

---

with the Father" borders dangerously on Monophysitism.

9. Ignatius offers numerous ancient creedal statements (e.g., *Eph.* 7.2; 18.2; *Magn.* 11.1; *Trall.* 9.1–2; *Smyrn.* 1.1–2), though lack of contemporary parallels leave one uncertain about the extent to which they are his own construction or reflect common confessions of the early Church.

10. See *CCC* 495, 497.

11. Supported secondarily by 1 Cor 2:8.

12. Not referenced in the *CCC*.

drew the image in comparison with the ancient Sybil).¹³ The editors instead retreat to later witnesses (Epiphanius and Clement of Alexandria) for support, pushing the convictions of the *Shepherd* no further, despite the author's obvious regard for this doctrine.

(d) *CCC* **830** returns to Ignatius for definition and use of the term "catholic/universal" (*katholikē*), here citing his words, "Where there is Jesus Christ, there is the Catholic Church" (*Smyrn.* 8.2). Within the AF only Ignatius and the *Martyrdom* (see proem; 8.1; 16.2; 19.2) make use of this word and, in the case of Ignatius, only here. One wonders why the *Martyrdom* is not cited, especially since it celebrates the bishop Polycarp of Smyrna, whose words are otherwise cited by the editors.[14] In truth, Polycarp seems to hold less inspiration for the editors, which may explain the omission of citations from the *Martyrdom*. Otherwise, Scripture is referenced as further description for the universal nature of the church (see Eph 1:22–23; Matt 28:19).

(e) *CCC* **834** returns to Ignatius in support of the specific nature of "catholic" churches in communion with Rome, "which presides in charity" (*prokathēmenē tēs agapes*; *Rom.* 1.1) versus other assemblies, according to the bishop. The editors read this phrase as indication of the centrality of the Roman Church, and Ignatius certainly applauds the value, success, and sanctification of that community in his epistle. No other mention of Rome's centrality appears in his writings, however, which raises some concern about his intentions or the authenticity of the text. Does he simply acknowledge Rome's influence or, perhaps more likely, his hope that Christians there will favor his cause?[15] The *CCC* does not debate this issue, leaving the question unexamined.

(f) *CCC* **861** brings the reader to a new source from Rome itself: *1 Clement* (42 and 44). These texts are not cited specifically, but are referenced secondarily in support of *Lumen gentium* 20. The author of *1 Clement* offers an ecclesiastical window into the view that gospel truth has been handed from "the Lord Jesus Christ" to the apostles to the bishops, an authority that the community in Corinth has seemingly neglected.[16] The editors offer

---

13. See Osiek, *Shepherd of Hermas*, 58.
14. See below *CCC* 1570 at #r.
15. Jefford, "Ignatius of Antioch and the Rhetoric of Christian Freedom," 25–39.
16. Lona, *Der erste Clemensbrief*, 455–81.

no Scripture as support,[17] though they might have appealed to the Ignatian view of "catholic" here. Thus *1 Clement* stands as the editors' oldest literary (and thus key) reference for the perspective.

(g) *CCC* 896 returns for a third time to Ignatius's epistle to Smyrna, in which he tenders advice about the need for laity to closely follow their leaders:

> Let all follow the bishop, as Jesus Christ follows his Father, and the college of presbyters as the apostles; respect the deacons as you do God's law. Let no one do anything concerning the Church in separation from the bishop. (*Smyrn.* 8.1)

The editors read Ignatius here in support of *Lumen gentium* 27: "[t]he faithful . . . should be closely attached to the bishop as the Church is to Jesus Christ, and as Jesus Christ is to the Father." This most important theme centers ecclesiastical authority around the bishop within each community, a figure whom Ignatius believes to be the presence of God. One could do no better than employ this particular source in support of such an observation.

(h) *CCC* 957 brings the *Martyrdom* into consideration, offering a view of the church's role as the communion of saints. This wording reads:

> We worship Christ as God's Son; we love the martyrs as the Lord's disciples and imitators, and rightly so because of their matchless devotion towards their king and master. May we also be their companions and fellow disciples! (*Mart.* 17.3)[18]

The editors offer this ancient sentiment as foundation for "the union of the whole Church in the Spirit," ultimately appealing to Eph 4:1–6 as the source of the conviction.

The context of the passage in the *Martyrdom* is somewhat polemical in that it is the author's confessional response against "the Evil One" (*ho ponēros*), who encouraged "the Jews" (*hoi Ioudaioi*) to bring Polycarp to his death, ultimately leading to the cremation of his bones. The author describes this event as the "birthday of his martyrdom" (*tēn tou martyriou*

---

17. Though one might extrapolate the idea from the selection of Matthias to fill the role of Judas in Acts 1:21–26, and especially of the author's reference to Ps 109:8 here: "let another take his office," or more literally, "let another receive his *episcopacy*" (*tēn episkopēn autou labetō heteros*).

18. The *CCC* lists this simply as *Mart.* 17. The word "master" (*didaskalon*) here is more commonly rendered "teacher."

autou hēmeran), thus initiating a practice by which the church celebrates the birth of martyrs.

(i) *CCC* 1010 offers the first of two Ignatian references from his epistle to Rome, each of which speaks about the nature of Christian death. Imagery is available from Scripture (see Phil 1:21; 2 Tim 2:11), but is no more vividly stated than here. One reads as follows:

> It is better for me to die in (*eis*) Christ Jesus than to reign over the ends of the earth. Him it is I seek—who died for us. Him it is I desire—who rose for us. I am on the point of giving birth . . . . Let me receive pure light; when I shall have arrived there, then shall I be a man. (*Rom.* 6.1–2)

With this citation the editors illustrate the nature of death as transformation through faith. The concluding words (translated here as "be a man" [*anthrōpos esomai*]) suggest elements of heroic achievement (through Christ), though one might with justification substitute the phrase "become human,"[19] thus to indicate that the full nature of human existence is achieved through participation in the mystery of Christ raised from the tomb. Regardless, Ignatius is the obvious choice for this sentiment.

(j) *CCC* 1011 continues with Ignatius's epistle to Rome, offering the following words: "My earthly desire has been crucified; . . . there is living water in me, water that murmurs and says within me: Come to the Father" (*Rom.* 7.2).[20] The phrase "earthly desire has been crucified" recalls the apostle Paul's phrasing, "the world has been crucified to me and I to the world" (Gal 6:14), though the Ignatian idiom "earthly desire" (*erōs*) points specifically to passion. The bishop speaks of the desire of "the ruler of this age" to take him captive and weaken his resolve, proffering enticements of corruptible pleasures. The editors see this in a different light, however, recalling the desire for death indicated by the apostle Paul as transformation into "an act of obedience . . . after the example of Christ" (Phil 1:23). In both instances the action of dying in Christ in order to achieve unity with the Father is offered as the most desirable goal of faith.

Summary: One finds these twelve references to be dominated by insights from Ignatius and his focus on the centrality of the bishop, universal church, and devotion that leads to sacrificial death. Allusions to *1 Clement*

---

19. Holmes, *The Apostolic Fathers*, 233.
20. Incorrectly attributed to *Rom.* 6.1–2.

and the *Martyrdom* appear as well, primarily in support of these same themes. Expressions of early Christian thought about the nature of Christ and governance of the church underscore the unified tradition, a lynchpin that holds all references together. Most important is the authority given to Ignatius as a figure whose remarks and creeds come close to bearing an authority similar to (though distinct from) Scripture.

The Celebration of the Christian Mystery

(k) *CCC* **1331** describes why the Eucharist is otherwise identified within the tradition as "holy communion." Three references to the AF are included, two from the *Didache* (9.5; 10.6) and one from Ignatius's epistle to the Ephesians (20.2). Providing as their primary referent certain foundational words from the apostle Paul (1 Cor 10:16–17), the editors observe that by this sacrament the faithful are joined with Christ. The foundation of the teaching thus is located within Scripture itself.

Use of the AF subsequently is seen only as secondary to the argument and here in a tenuous fashion at best. The editors designate the Eucharist as "the holy things" (*ta hagia*; *sancta*), drawing support for this idea from the fourth-century *Apostolic Constitutions and Canons* (see 8.13.12). Here the two *Didache* texts are included as auxiliary evidence, which is curious since the Didachist makes no use of the words "the holy things" at these places and may actually have some other liturgical event in mind.[21] This is a matter of debate, but one must at least acknowledge that no attempt has been made to incorporate the so-called words of institution into this narrative or to associate the event with the sacrificial death of Christ.

Otherwise, Ignatius's now famous phrase "medicine of immortality" is included as an apt description of the Eucharist now found within the Apostle's Creed. Ignatius indicates that the Eucharist is an "antidote" (*antidotos*) by which the faithful may avoid death and receive life in Christ. The allusion is most fitting within the secondary context of the *CCC*.

(l) *CCC* **1369** offers further direction with respect to the role of the bishop in the celebration of the Eucharist. Following the instructions of Ignatius, the editors quote from his epistle to the Smyrnaeans:

---

21. Betz, "The Eucharist in the Didache," 244–75.

> Let only that Eucharist be regarded as legitimate, which is celebrated under the [presidency of] the bishop or him to whom he has entrusted it. (*Smyrn.* 8.1)

By virtue of tradition this authority is associated specifically with the pope, "[s]ince he has the ministry of Peter in the Church." Ignatius himself makes no such claim, conceding the grandeur of the Roman Church in his epistle to the Romans, but otherwise offering no allusion to the unique nature of the episcopal office there either by name or position or by making mention of Roman hegemony elsewhere among his epistles. In this respect tradition has expanded the Ignatian vision beyond its original parameters.

(m) *CCC* 1403 returns to *Did.* 10.6, a text already employed in secondary (and somewhat dubious) fashion in *CCC* 1391.[22] Here the words of the Lord at the Last Supper are recalled from Scripture with respect to that time when he will drink the fruit of the vine in his Father's kingdom (Matt 26:29 pars.), thus recalling the church's proclamation "maranatha" (1 Cor 16:22; Rev 1:4; 22:20). Similar wording appears in *Did.* 10.6, associated with the phrase (as recalled by the *CCC*) "May your grace come and this world pass away!" The possessive "your" is not actually supported by manuscripts for the *Didache*, and its inclusion offers significant alteration to the passage, since the Didachist likely speaks of God the Father, while the editors (by virtue of their quotation "Come, Lord Jesus" immediately preceding) clearly associate the proclamation with the mind of Christ and the salvific nature of the Eucharist that he directed his disciples to proclaim. To include the *Didache* as support for the church's confession is thus not unwarranted, but its emended citation brings fresh vision that is more in keeping with the contemporary expression of tradition than was likely intended originally.

(n) *CCC* 1405 returns to Ignatius and his epistle to Ephesus. Use of Ignatius here is primarily descriptive, offering further characterization for the nature of the Eucharist: "We break the one bread that provides the medicine of immortality, the antidote for death, and the food that makes us live for ever in Jesus Christ" (*Eph.* 20.2). These words on the Eucharist provide special prominence to the bishop's instruction by virtue of their role as the section's conclusion.

---

22. See above *CCC* 1331 at #k.

(o) *CCC* 1432 features a return to *1 Clement* in which one finds a discussion of penance. This brief paragraph describes the weighty nature of human sin and the opportunity for conversion when Christ is encountered. Thus one reads:

> Let us fix our eyes on Christ's blood and understand how precious it is to his Father, for, poured out for our salvation, it has brought to the whole world the grace of repentance. (*1 Clem.* 7.4)

Use of this work from the AF is appropriate, since the author at Rome seeks to encourage the community at Corinth to recognize its folly in replacing worthy elders with younger upstarts.[23] The editors transfer the context, however, moving from general community appeal toward individual devotion, thus to make the charge more personal in nature. This transition offers support for Scripture used earlier in the passage (Ezek 36:26–27; Lam 5:21; John 19:37; Zech 12:10).

(p) *CCC* 1549 returns to Ignatius, employing two separate epistles: *Trall.* 3.1 and *Magn.* 6.1.[24] Of concern is the person of Christ as head of the church, an image that "is made visible" to the community through bishops and priests. Specifically, the bishop is identified as *typos tou Patros* (so *Trall.* 3.1), read literally as "image of the Father," but which is otherwise difficult to translate in any distinctly meaningful sense. The editors identify the phrase with "the living image of God the Father," presumably to reflect the secondary attribution of *Magn.* 6.1, though here Ignatius employs the words "the bishop presiding in the place of God" (*prokathēmenou tou episkopou eis topon theou*). He undoubtedly would agree with such a characterization of bishops, though this particular wording is not employed in either passage.

(q) *CCC* 1554 returns to Ignatius's epistle to Tralles to discuss the sacrament of holy orders. Here the editors quote the bishop in full:

> Let everyone revere the deacons as Jesus Christ, the bishop as the image of the Father, and the presbyters as the senate of God and the assembly of the apostles. For without them one cannot speak of the Church. (*Trall.* 3.1)[25]

---

23. Bowe, *A Church in Crisis*, 7–32.
24. See below *CCC* 1554 and 1593 at #q and t respectively.
25. For the concept of bishop as image of the Father, see above *CCC* 1549 at #p.

What is not addressed by this citation is the very point the editors seek to affirm about the "two degrees of ministerial participation in the priesthood of Christ: the episcopacy and the presbyterate," who are assisted in their role by the deacons. Ignatius suggests instead that, while the bishop reflects the "image of the Father" and the presbyters that of the "senate of God" (*synedrios theou*) and "assembly of the apostles" (*syndesmos apostolōn*), Jesus Christ stands in the role of the diaconate. Thus, use of the term *sacerdos* to denote bishops and priests but not deacons is not so readily supported by the Ignatian vision. This awkward wording is occasionally revised in manuscript renderings of the passage, thus to indicate some discomfort with the bishop's perspective. Otherwise, one seeks another explanation, such as to argue that Ignatius's "choice of language here was probably determined by the immediate context" about the significance of the role of deacons for his audience.[26] Regardless, the Ignatian image as derived from this passage remains awkward for the editors' argument.

(r) *CCC* 1570 turns to the editors' only use of materials from the bishop Polycarp (contemporary of Ignatius) and here simply to support the gospel witness. The discussion concerns the ordination of deacons and their nature as servants, finding its primary witness in the model of Christ himself, who is characterized as "the one who serves" (*hōs ho diakonōn*; so Luke 22:27; cf. Mark 10:45). As provision for this description, the editors offer Polycarp's *Phil.* 5.2, an observation by the bishop that deacons must be "servants of God and Christ and not of people" (*hōs theou kai Xristou diakonoi kai ouk anthrōpōn*). Polycarp's admonition supports the editors' reading only in part, encouraging deacons at Philippi to serve God and Christ (so the *CCC*) but admonishing them *not* to serve people (contrary to the words of the gospels that Christ came specifically *in order to* serve others; Matt 20:28 pars.). One can hardly deny that Polycarp was likely unopposed to diaconate service on behalf of the needs of the church and its people, though here his language suggests a different focus as he attempts to identify the true nature of what it means to be a deacon.[27] Otherwise, it is curious that only in this single instance is Polycarp employed by the editors, since he clearly was a well-revered figure of early Christian prominence.[28]

---

26. Schoedel, *Ignatius of Antioch*, 141.

27. Hartog, *Polycarp's* Epistle to the Philippians *and the* Martyrdom of Polycarp, 119–21.

28. The editors could have returned to Ignatius, *Trall.* 3.1 here (see above *CCC* 1554 at #q) since, supported by passages from Mark and Luke, the bishop specifically associates

(s) ***CCC* 1577** turns once again to *1 Clement* with respect to those who may receive the sacrament of holy orders. Two texts are used (42.4; 44.3), both offered in secondary support of various New Testament passages (Mark 3:14–19; Luke 6:12–16; 1 Tim 3:1–13; 2 Tim 1:6), and these are seen to reflect ancient tradition.[29] The passages provide a general basis for the editors' observation that "[t]he Lord Jesus chose men (*viri*) to form the college of the twelve apostles, and the apostles did the same when they chose collaborators to succeed them in their ministry."[30] The wording from *1 Clement* offers backing for the latter portion of the observation, namely, that the apostles themselves appointed "men" (*androi*) as bishops and deacons to succeed them, though only 44.3 stipulates specifically that those who were chosen were male. Claims for apostolic succession are not available in the AF apart from *1 Clement*, thus to make it a suitable choice for these observations.

(t) ***CCC* 1593** offers a third use of Ignatius's epistle to the Trallians (*Trall.* 3.1) and the final appearance of the AF in the discussion on Christian Mystery. Here a brief repetition of the statement in the *CCC* confirms the tripartite division of clerical organization among the offices of bishop, presbyter, and deacon.[31] Ignatius alone provides the most obvious support for this perspective, a conviction that has become foundational for later views about the nature of ecclesiastical offices. This is both consoling and vexing, since one hopes to find other evidence to support the Ignatian perspective within the AF if the bishop's views were typical of his day. Otherwise, one might argue that this vision was singular to Ignatius and not shared by his contemporaries.[32] In either case, there is no question that his views are bedrock for later ecclesiastical leadership.

Summary: As with the first section on Profession of Faith, one again discovers preference for the teachings of Ignatius as a standard by which to define offices of the church and the nature of those who serve in these roles. Quick reference to the *Didache*, *1 Clement*, and Polycarp's epistle to Philippi holds lesser importance. Only the support of *1 Clement* has any meaningful place in this discussion, since that text likewise endorses apostolic succession. Primary among usages of the AF is Ignatius, *Trall.* 3.1 with respect to

---

Christ with the role of deacon.

29. Bowe, *A Church in Crisis*, 142–53.
30. It is unclear why Matt 10:1–4 is not offered as further support.
31. See above *CCC* 1554 at #q.
32. Brent, *Ignatius of Antioch and the Second Sophistic*, 23–30, 313.

tripartite division of clerical offices as reflection of divine attributes, reconfirming the role that the bishop himself holds for tradition.

Life in Christ

(u) *CCC* **1696** turns to *Did.* 1.2 among its opening words on Christian living, drawing on the ancient "two ways" teaching known from Scripture (cf. Deut 30:14–20; Matt 7:13; Jer 21:8; Prov 12:28; Sir 15:17; Gal 5:17–18). The text is quoted in full: "There are two ways, the one of life, the other of death; but between the two, there is a great difference" (cf. *Barn.* 18.1; Herm. *Mand.* 6.1.1—6.2.10). The editors apply this teaching specifically to "the importance of moral decisions for our salvation," though one might imagine that more than morality is at stake in the original contexts for this instruction. Regardless, this foundational admonition is an appropriate element of the editors' directives, even as it was viewed as worthy introduction by the Didachist.

(v) *CCC* **1900** returns to the topic of social life with a long quotation from *1 Clement*. The citation is introduced with the words "Pope St. Clement of Rome provides the Church's most ancient prayer for political authorities," recalling by comparison the instruction to pray for leaders in positions of high authority found in 1 Tim 2:1–2 (a text that the editors observe in comparison to be as old as the Clementine reference).[33] Thereafter, the passage reads as follows:

> Grant to them, Lord, health, peace, concord, and stability, so that they may exercise without offense the sovereignty that you have given them. Master, heavenly King of the ages, you give glory, honor, and power over the things of earth to the sons of men. Direct, Lord, their counsel, following what is pleasing and acceptable in your sight, so that by exercising with devotion and in peace and gentleness the power that you have given to them, they may find favor with you. (*1 Clem.* 61.1b–2)[34]

---

33. This creates an interesting situation, since it assumes *1 Clement* either to be early (60s–70s), which is not a traditional view, or closer to the end of the century (90s). In neither case is the apostle Paul likely affirmed as the author of 1 Timothy, however, since the former date suggests he was *not* martyred in Rome in the 60s and the latter is beyond the scope of his lifetime.

34. Listed simply as *1 Clem* 61 in the notes.

Appeals to *1 Clement* are appropriate here, both for its use of early Christian prayer and insight into interaction between the church and secular authority. The AF are again utilized to support what Scripture has rendered previously (Rom 13:1–2; 1 Pet 2:13–17).

(w) CCC 1905 provides occasion to incorporate the text of *Barnabas*, this being the first of two usages in the text.[35] The passage concludes discussion about the common good: "Do not live entirely isolated, having retreated into yourselves, as if you were already justified, but gather instead to seek the common good together" (*Barn.* 4.10). The citation as applied to daily living is intriguing, since the author of *Barnabas* specifically warns here against the faithful isolating themselves "in the last days" (*en tais eschatais hēmerais*) without reference to day-to-day activities such as the editors assume. In fact, *Barnabas* continues with a quotation from LXX Isa 5:21 ("woe to those who are wise in their own opinion and clever in their own eyes") and says "let us become spiritual ones" (*genōmetha pneumatikoi*) in an effort to warn against "an over-realised eschatology" with respect to life in Christ.[36] As with the editors' employment of Ignatius elsewhere in the *CCC*,[37] original context holds little relevance for the discussion.

(x) CCC 2175 incorporates the words of Ignatius once again, returning to his epistle to the Magnesians. Here the editors speak about the importance of the Christian sabbath, Sunday:

> Those who lived according to the old order of things have come to a new hope, no longer keeping the sabbath, but the Lord's Day, in which our life is blessed by him and by his death. (*Magn.* 9.1)

Ignatius only uses the phrase "the Lord's Day" (*kyriakē*) in this passage, which otherwise finds rare parallel in Rev 1:10 ("on the Lord's day"; *en tē kyriakē*) and *Did.* 14.1 ("on the Lord's own day"; *kata kyriakēn de kyriou*). Undoubtedly the editors correctly use the expression in reference to Sunday (a later Christian designation for first day of the week), though literary evidence suggests its use primarily in Asia Minor and Syria, and there is no reason to think that believers in the late first and early second centuries (being largely from Jewish backgrounds) did not also continue to observe their own traditional sabbath days of worship.

---

35. See below *CCC* 2271 at #z.
36. Carleton Paget, *The Epistle of Barnabas*, 113.
37. See above *CCC* 496 and 498 at #a and b respectively.

(y) ***CCC* 2240** includes three citations from *Diognetus*, each devoted to the topic of duty of citizens. These observations derive their foundation from Scripture (Rom 13:1–2; 1 Pet 2:13, 16; 1 Tim 2:2)[38] and are linked together by the editors as a single passage:

> [Christians] reside in their own nations, but as resident aliens. They participate in all things as citizens and endure all things as foreigners. . . . They obey the established laws and their way of life surpasses the laws. . . . So noble is the position to which God has assigned them that they are not allowed to desert it. (*Diogn.* 5.5, 10; 6.10)

The admonitions of Scripture to support traditions of honor and authority are elsewhere supported in the AF at *1 Clem.* 2.8 and *Mart.* 13.2. Such texts (though not used here) help to define the true intention of *Diognetus*, that is, authentic Christian lifestyle does not separate itself from traditional canons of ethics and morality. To the extent that the editors recognize this reality in these paragraphs, they correctly employ the intention of the biblical authors and AF. Use of these sources to endorse activities by secular authorities *de facto*, however, is surely a misreading of the early Christian witness.

(z) ***CCC* 2271** brings the reader to the topic of abortion, again offering support from texts of the AF, though here without explicit foundation in Scripture. Only one of three passages is cited, that of *Did.* 2.2: "You shall not kill the embryo by abortion and shall not cause the newborn to perish." The Didachist offers this teaching as partial support for the Decalogue's prohibition against murder, listing it among sins that new Christians must avoid as part of an appropriate lifestyle. *Barn.* 19.5 has an exact parallel to the words of the *Didache*, though not necessarily as catechetical instruction for new Christians. In both instances the authors include these words as explanation for the "two ways" of life. A third passage found at *Diogn.* 5.6 says about Christians that they "have children but do not expose their offspring." This late second-century source decries a practice employed by pagans who, wishing to be rid of newborns, would leave them to be exposed to the elements, savaged by animals, or acquired by slave traders.

This paragraph betrays the importance of the AF for the editors beyond that of the bishop Ignatius himself, providing through special example an instance in which the authors of three other texts (the *Didache*,

---

38. One wonders why Paul's words on "citizenship/commonwealth" (*politeia, politeuma*) are not further employed; see Phil 3:20.

Barnabas, and *Diognetus*) serve as foundational sources for key traditions of the church, in this case the nature of life. In certain respects this usage is unique for the editors, since otherwise these authors hold limited interest for them. More notably, one sees the importance of non-canonical literature for church teaching when Scripture is not available.

(aa) CCC 2473 once more returns to Ignatius and his epistle to Rome in which he attests to the power of martyrdom as a witness to truth. The editors quote here: "Let me become the food of the beasts, through whom it will be given me to reach God" (*Rom.* 4.1). The act of martyrdom is envisaged as "the supreme witness" that demonstrates "the truth of the faith and of Christian doctrine," and in this respect Ignatius has traditionally been recognized as an exemplar by which other believers may be measured.

(ab) CCC 2474 observes that the church reveres those who are martyred and preserves literary evidence of their accounts. The editors continue with the Ignatian epistle to Rome, as well as reference to Polycarp's execution as depicted in the *Martyrdom*. Relevant passages read as follows:

> Neither the pleasures of the world nor the kingdoms of this age will be of any use to me. It is better for me to die [in order to unite myself] to Christ Jesus than to reign over the ends of the earth. I seek him who died for us; I desire him who rose for us. My birth is approaching.... (*Rom.* 6.1–2)[39]

> I bless you for having judged me worthy from this day and this hour to be counted among your martyrs.... You have kept your promise, God of faithfulness and truth. For this reason and for everything, I praise you, I bless you, I glorify you through the eternal and heavenly High Priest, Jesus Christ, your beloved Son. Through him, who is with you and the Holy Spirit, may glory be given to you, now and in the ages to come. Amen. (*Mart.* 14.2–3)

Both references contain a confessional aspect. The Ignatian text anticipates martyrdom and defines the nature of death as new "birth" in terms thereafter used by the church to indicate the birth of a martyr (cf. *Mart.* 18.3). The rendering of Polycarp's prayer is highly trinitarian in nature ("God of faithfulness ... Jesus Christ your beloved Son ... the Holy Spirit), which is not always evident elsewhere in the AF. Each quotation provides witness to

---

39. See above CCC 1010 at #i.

the strength of faith in confrontation with persecution, as the editors say, "written in letters of blood."

(ac) *CCC* **2517** returns to the *Shepherd* for the second (and final) use of that text and last appearance of the AF in this section. The sin of covetousness is addressed with broad comment: "Remain simple and innocent, and you will be like little children who do not know the evil that destroys man's life" (Herm. *Mand.* 2.1). This advice is worthy in context, but the author of the *Shepherd* does not apply it to this same issue, choosing instead to warn that one should not speak evil of others, hold a grudge, or be slanderous. The comment is linked by the editors with "purifying the heart and practicing temperance," which otherwise reflects the words of Jesus (Matt 15:19): "Out of the heart come evil thoughts, murder, adultery, fornication. . . ." (cf. Exod 20:7–17; Deut 5:7–21). One may thus argue that as a general observation the words are well placed, even if they are offered apart from the original context.

Summary: Again one finds here a broad dependence on Ignatius intermingled with sporadic use of other authorities on a limited basis. The "two ways" tradition finds ready use here, together with creedal prayers from *1 Clement*, Ignatius, and Polycarp. Most important for tradition is the comment on abortion, whose ultimate source is the *Didache* and *Barnabas*. The text of *Diognetus* also is prominent beyond any consideration for its use elsewhere in the *CCC*. For the topic of life in Christ, the witness of the AF is entirely appropriate for tradition.

Christian Prayer

(ad) *CCC* **2760** is the second paragraph of Section Two on the Lord's Prayer, where the editors cite *Did.* 8.2 ("For yours are the power and the glory for ever") as early support for a doxological closing to the prayer.[40] Apart from several manuscripts that support the phrasing elsewhere in Matt 6:9–12, this is the oldest non-canonical use of the wording. Yet it is not entirely clear that this conclusion was original to the *Didache* (dated to the late first or early second centuries), and so the entire prayer may be secondary to the original creation of the text.[41] As the text now stands, the editors are correct

---

40. Supplemented with the words "the kingdom" at the beginning from *Apostolic Constitutions and Canons* 7.24.1.

41. Pardee, *The Genre and Development of the* Didache, 185, 190.

in their attribution of the doxology to an ancient context, but with respect to scholarly deliberation the point may be moot.

(ae) *CCC* **2767** continues with use of the *Didache*, incorporating instruction from *Did.* 8.3 to pray the Lord's Prayer three times a day. This likely represents an attempt by the Didachist to circumvent traditional practices of Jewish piety, which the editors identify specifically as the "Eighteen Benedictions," though this comparison remains unsubstantiated. In any case, it is clear that early Christians received training with respect to alternative customs of devotion (in comparison to Jewish and pagan practices) and that the *Didache* attests to this reality.

(af) *CCC* **2796** offers the last use of *Diognetus* in which the spiritual nature of those who confess the faith is defined: "[Christians] are in the flesh, but do not live according to the flesh. They spend their lives on earth, but are citizens of heaven" (*Diogn.* 5.8–9). This citation already finds scriptural foundation beyond the Lord's Prayer in Matthew (cf. 2 Cor 5:2; Phil 3:20; Heb 13:14) and serves as the editors' closing comments on the phrase "our Father who art in heaven." The reference is pertinent, even though not applied to the prayer in this context by *Diognetus*.

(ag) *CCC* **2837** offers the final reference to the AF, once more making use of Ignatius's phrase "medicine of immorality" (*Eph.* 20.2),[42] though here with specific reference to "Bread of Life, the Body of Christ" as the image to which the term "daily" (*epiousios*) in the phrase "give us this day our daily bread" alludes. The qualitative rationale for this interpretation is drawn from Scripture (1 Tim 6:8), while further support for the editors' reading comes from later patristic sources.[43] In context the Ignatian reference defines the phrase "breaking one bread" (*hena arton klōntes*), a clear reference to Eucharistic practices in the early church. While Ignatius himself does not employ the Lord's Prayer for examination in this regard, the Didachist *does* offer the prayer,[44] but unfortunately provides no interpretation to support tradition's reading here.

Summary: In this final brief section four usages from the AF are found (two from the *Didache*, one from *Diognetus*, and yet another from Ignatius), all of which are applied to an examination of the Lord's Prayer as

---

42. See above *CCC* 1331 and 1405 at #k and n respectively.
43. Augustine, *Sermo* 57.7; Peter Chrysologus, *Sermo* 67.
44. See above *CCC* 2760 at #ad.

employed in the church's life of devotion. The voice of Ignatius is retained, yet it is no longer the dominant guide. The issue of prayer and praying is widespread throughout the AF, and one might have expected parallels from *1 Clement*, Polycarp, and the *Martyrdom* as further support for the editors' comments. But at the end of the day these are seen as unnecessary to sustain the analysis, and thus remain beyond the discussion.

Conclusions

This review of citations in which the *CCC* has incorporated the AF leads to several preliminary conclusions. These apply only to the editors' use of the AF, not necessarily to editorial technique otherwise.

From the outset the AF are employed both as support for biblical texts or in lieu of them. On the one hand, numerous passages appear as backing for Scripture (cf. #d, h–k, m, o, r–s, v, y, ac–ad, af); on the other, the AF often stand as their own source of authority apart from canon (cf. #b–c, e–g, l, n, p–q, t, x, z, aa–ab). A few cases do not seem to fit either category, blending Scripture with the AF without concern for primacy of authority (cf. #a, u, w, ae). The general division between dependence on and independence from Scripture suggests that the editors find little actual distinction between the two sets of materials, signifying that the designation *canon* holds no critical meaning here. Thus, if Scripture can serve as foundation for an argument, then it is accepted; if no Scripture is available, then the AF serve as suitable substitute.

Second, while the AF bear authority deemed similar to Scripture, they themselves are not equivalent in value. Some authors are omitted altogether (*2 Clement*, Papias), while others serve a minimal role at best, namely, *Barnabas* (cf. #w, z), the *Shepherd* (cf. #c, ac), and the Polycarp tradition (cf. #h, r, ab). Of the remaining sources, *Diognetus* (cf. #y–z, af), *1 Clement* (cf. #f, o, s, v), and the *Didache* (cf. #k, m, u, z, ad–ae) receive more attention, though mostly in minor capacities. The favorite source above all others is the bishop Ignatius, whose comments and imagery govern the editors' comments. His influence is evident throughout all four sections (cf. #a–b, d–e, g, i–l, n, p–q, t, x, aa–ab, ag), which suggests that his insights, creeds, and convictions about ecclesiastical orders and the meaning of Eucharist are foundational for tradition at large. In result, one might offer that Roman Catholicism may with some justification be categorized as Ignatian catholicism.

Third, the editors have sometimes accepted elements of ancient tradition as customary practice within early Christianity when only mentioned once within the AF, in most cases associated with the views of Ignatius. This seems true in at least two contexts, namely, the editors' comment on the centrality of Rome (cf. #e) and the tripartite division of clerical offices (cf. #t). These are delicate issues for tradition, and there is no particular reason to think that the foundation of either conviction is not ancient. One simply observes with respect to traditions preserved by the church that what is typically accepted as broad practice can in fact only be offered with limited literary substantiation.

Fourth, original contexts have little concern for the editors. This is not unexpected, since the same has been true for Christian authors from the beginning, evidenced already in the use of Jewish scriptures by those who wrote the New Testament. One finds examples of contextual myopia in scattered locations (cf. #a–b, h, m, o, r, u, w, ac), including themes related to Ignatius's view of Jesus's conception and the "three mysteries worthy of proclamation," the objection of the *Martyrdom* to "the Evil One," the Didachist's orientation toward the Father (versus Christ) in the Lord's Prayer, Polycarp's concern that deacons serve with Christ as models, and the orientation of *Barnabas* toward living "in the last days." Change of context in the *CCC* typically is not dramatic and serves primarily to make teachings applicable to contemporary context. Nevertheless, it is useful to be aware of these subtle shifts in presentation.

Finally, examples from the AF are occasionally drawn from the most obvious expressions of certain themes without consideration of other materials that would support the topic at hand. For example, when the *Shepherd* is invoked to back the conviction that the church is eternal (cf. #c), extra illustration from 2 *Clem.* 14.1–5 is ignored. When Ignatian use of "catholic/universal" is celebrated as typical of the early church's self-understanding (cf. #d), usages from the *Martyrdom* that exemplify that identity go unheeded. When Ignatius is employed as evidence of Roman hegemony via the apostolic lineage of the apostle Peter, similar claims from *1 Clement* (a text written from a central position of authority) go unnoticed (see *1 Clem.* 5.3–4). Finally, when the editors draw on *Diognetus* to discuss the legitimate nature of secular authority (cf. #y), further evidence from *1 Clem.* 2.8 and *Mart.* 13.2 is overlooked. Such omissions are not necessarily problematic, but their inclusion typically would have strengthened the editors' point.

In the final analysis one can perhaps now understand how a set of early Christian materials such as the AF (of which most readers are uninformed) sometimes serves a key role for how the editors of the *CCC* can support key confessions of the tradition. Neither defined as Scripture nor viewed as classic patristic teaching, the AF stand in an ill-defined role between canon and doctrine, yet serve as foundation for important teachings related to the eternal nature of the church, tripartite division of clerical offices, primacy of Rome, centrality of the Lord's Prayer, prohibition of abortion, and other such matters. This small collection of texts has impacted tradition, especially through the figure of the bishop Ignatius, though it is often taken lightly. Here is literary witness to the post-apostolic faith of the church's foundation, a platform for what tradition teaches today. Here are two sides of a coin by which the faith is often defined: true witness and firm conviction.

Readers of the *CCC* are well advised to recognize the presence of the AF in the course of their reflections on this important ecclesiastical document. Its foundations are firmly rooted in the confessional experience of the ancient church. Its teachings reflect the experiences of those who have come before our present generation. Its insights contribute greatly to the educational development of all who seek further understanding within the faith tradition. It is through such sources as the AF that we come to educate ourselves about how what we believe about daily Christian living is supported by what we know about the ancient faith itself. This literature should certainly not be neglected.

Bibliography

Betz, Johannes. "The Eucharist in the Didache." In *The Didache in Modern Research*, edited by Jonathan A. Draper, 244–75. Arbeiten zur Geschichte des antiken Judentums und des Urchristentums 37. Leiden: Brill, 1996.

Bowe, Barbara Ellen. *A Church in Crisis: Ecclesiology and Paraenesis in Clement of Rome*. Harvard Dissertations in Religion 23. Minneapolis: Fortress, 1998.

Brent, Allen. *Ignatius of Antioch and the Second Sophistic*. Studien und Texte zu Antike und Christentum 36. Tübingen: Mohr Siebeck, 2006.

Carleton Paget, James. *The Epistle of Barnabas*. Wissenschaftliche Untersuchungen zum Neuen Testament 2, 64. Tübingen: J. C. B. Mohr (Paul Siebeck), 1994.

Foster, Paul, ed. *The Writings of the Apostolic Fathers*. T&T Clark Biblical Studies. New York and London: T. & T. Clark, 2007.

Gnuse, Robert Karl. *No Other Gods: Emergent Monotheism in Israel*. Journal of Old Testament Studies 241. Sheffield: Sheffield Academic, 1997.

Günther, Matthias. *Einleitung in die Apostolischen Väter*. Arbeiten zur Religion und Geschichte des Urchristentums 4. Frankfurt am Main: Peter Lang, 1997.

Hartog, Paul, ed. *Polycarp's* Epistle to the Philippians *and the* Martyrdom of Polycarp. Oxford Apostolic Fathers. Oxford: Oxford University Press, 2013.

Holmes, Michael W. *The Apostolic Fathers: Greek Texts and English Translations*. 3rd ed. Grand Rapids: Baker Academic, 2007.

Jefford, Clayton N. "Ignatius of Antioch and the Rhetoric of Christian Freedom." In *Christian Freedom*, edited by Clayton N. Jefford, 25–39. American University Studies 7/Theology and Religion 144. New York: Peter Lang, 1993.

———. *Reading the Apostolic Fathers*. 2nd ed. Grand Rapids: Baker Academic, 2012.

Lona, Horacio E. *Der erste Clemensbrief*. Kommentar zu den Apostolischen Vätern 2. Göttingen: Vandenhoeck & Ruprecht, 1998.

Osiek, Carolyn. *Shepherd of Hermas*. Hermeneia. Minneapolis: Fortress, 1999.

Pardee, Nancy. *The Genre and Development of the Didache*. Wissenschaftliche Untersuchungen zum Neuen Testament 2/339. Tübingen: Mohr Siebeck, 2012.

Pratscher, Wilhelm, ed. *The Apostolic Fathers*. Translated by Elisabeth G. Wolfe. Waco, TX: Baylor University Press, 2010.

Schoedel, William R. *Ignatius of Antioch*. Hermeneia. Philadelphia: Fortress, 1985.

2

"The Mystery Meaning You"
Augustine's Mystagogical Preaching
on the Church as the Body of Christ

—Kimberly F. Baker

Introduction

FOR AUGUSTINE OF HIPPO, the question of Catholic identity has a clear, positive answer. Augustine boldly joins the identity of Christ, the sacrament of the Eucharist, and the Church into one identity: that of Christ.[1] While this identity runs throughout his writings, it appears prominently in his preaching to the newly baptized. There, he proclaims without any hesitation that in baptism, these Christians received a new identity, the identity of Christ. Thus, they should recognize themselves on the altar in the consecrated bread, which has become the body of Christ:

> If you want to understand the body of Christ, listen to the apostle telling the faithful, *You, though, are the body of Christ and its members* (1 Cor 12:27). So if it's you that are the body of Christ and its members, it's the mystery meaning you that has been placed on the Lord's table; what you receive is the mystery that means you.

---

1. I have capitalized the word "Church" when referring to the Church in relation to Christ, except in direct quotes that use the lower-case, in order to express the personal, relational identity of the Church in Augustine's theology. Likewise, I have capitalized "Body of Christ" when it refers to the Church and its relation to Christ, its Head.

> It is to what you are that you reply, *Amen*, and by so replying you express your assent.[2]

To see Christ, he tells the assembly, look at the bread and wine on the altar ... and see yourself.

While he is known primarily for his treatises, preaching serves as Augustine's primary means for educating Christians about their religious identity and the transformation it brings. In his sermons, Augustine speaks with great clarity on Catholic identity, which for him would mean Christian identity in general since he understood "Catholic" in its root sense of universal or as he often puts it, the Church spread throughout the world. At the center of Augustine's conviction lies his doctrine of the *totus Christus*, the whole Christ with Christ as Head and the Church as Body. He takes seriously Paul's language of the Church as the Body of Christ, finding there not a metaphor but a reality. He teaches that the union of Christ and the Church is so total and complete that they can no longer be understood apart from one another. In the union of the *totus Christus*, Christ and the Church share one life, one identity. All other considerations of the Christian identity and life flow from this core identity of Christ.

In this chapter, I explore Augustine's preaching on the *totus Christus* to consider how he teaches and forms Christians in their identity in Christ. I approach this preaching as mystagogical catechesis that shapes a sacramental awareness reaching beyond the sacraments to the Church itself. I begin with an introduction to Augustine's doctrine of the *totus Christus*, initiated in the Incarnation. Then, I turn to the sacramental incorporation of Christians into this shared life with Christ and ways the life of the Church makes manifest this new life in Christ, finding that for Augustine, it is love, or *caritas*, that serves as the sign of one's identity in Christ. I conclude that Augustine's preaching on the *totus Christus* serves as on-going mystagogy and formation that extends beyond the Easter season to the broad life of the Church. Throughout the chapter, I show that in his preaching on the doctrine of the *totus Christus*, Augustine integrates Christ, sacrament, and Church into one life of love such that where one sees the Church, one can see Christ. Thus, the Church's identity in Christ is a sacramental reality that makes manifest the presence of Christ in the world.

---

2. Augustine, *Serm.* 272 (WSA 3/7:300).

The *Totus Christus*

Augustine's doctrine of the *totus Christus* places Christian identity firmly in the person of Christ. This doctrine emerged early in Augustine's preaching, beginning as a method for reading Scripture and developing into a central theme of his theology. After being chosen by popular acclaim for ordination as a presbyter in the North African city of Hippo in 391, Augustine steeped himself in an intensive study of the epistles of Paul, seeking biblical grounding for his ministry. He then put Paul's teaching of the Church as the Body of Christ to good use when preaching on the Psalms as he worked through his exegetical challenges with the assembly. Thus, he educated them not only in the doctrine but also in his theological method. In this process, he sought to form and nurture their Christian identity in Christ.

Convinced that the words of the Psalms should be heard as the words of Christ, he faced a challenge in explaining how Christ could speak of his sin, despair, and suffering. Aided by a handbook of biblical "rules" written by Tyconius,[3] he said that Christ speaks in union with the Church, his Body. At times, he speaks from his vantage point as Head of the Body, at other times in solidarity with his Body, the Church, in its own struggles, and at times, the two speak together. This method leads Augustine to think more deeply about the union of Christ and the Church until he comes to understand the two to be so united that they actually speak as one. He will go even further to say that they not only speak as one but share one life, one identity, that of Christ. Christology and ecclesiology merge as Augustine asserts that Christ and the Church share a deep, unbreakable union so complete that they cannot be understood apart from one another.

Augustine roots this union in the transformative love that led Christ to choose to unite with humanity in the Incarnation. This choice has lasting effects for both Christ and for humanity through the Church. In his study of Augustine's theology, Tarsicius van Bavel explains that Christ and the Church both receive their identity in the union of the *totus Christus*. Christ's identity comes from his choice to identify completely with humanity such that he experienced the needs and sufferings of humanity and continues to do so even from his place in heaven. Humanity's identification with Christ comes as a result of Christ's choice. Those who respond to Christ participate in his life and thus share his identity by entering the

---

3. Tyconius was a fourth-century Donatist lay theologian. His *Book of Rules* suggests that Scripture has seven "rules" that shape it and that understanding the rules can help to open the meaning of Scripture to the reader.

union in the Church.[4] Augustine uses bridal imagery to describe the union of Christ and the Church as so complete that the two have become one: one flesh, one voice, one identity as Christ. Even within this union, though, they retain their distinct roles, with Christ offering salvation and the Church receiving salvation.[5] Nonetheless, the two speak as one.

The doctrine of the *totus Christus* appears frequently in Augustine's preaching, whether explicitly or implicitly. As his own understanding of the relation of Christ and the Church deepens, so too do his sermons call the community to a deeper understanding of their identity and life in Christ. A sermon on the Psalms offers the assembly a summary of the doctrine: "But in fact he who deigned to assume the form of a slave, and within that form to clothe us with himself, he who did not disdain to take us up into himself, did not disdain either to transfigure us into himself, and to speak in our words, so that we in our turn might speak in his."[6] Christ and humanity share a voice, speak in the words of one another, as a result of Christ's initiative in the Incarnation. The union endures after Christ's ascension into heaven, as Augustine says a few lines later: "The whole Christ consists of Head and body. The Head is he who is the savior of his body, he who has already ascended into heaven; but the body is the Church, toiling on earth."[7]

One could say that the Church extends the Incarnation as Christ continues to identify so completely with the Church that he is present in the world in the Church. Augustine often refers to Christ's cry from heaven in Acts 9:4 as evidence that Christ continues to suffer in solidarity with the Church: "Were it not for the body's linkage with its Head through the bond of charity, so close a link that Head and body speak as one, he could not have rebuked a certain persecutor from heaven with the question, *Saul, Saul, why are you persecuting me?* (Acts 9:4)."[8] Love forms the bond of Christ and the Church, drawing Christ to humanity in the first place and sealing his union with the Church. This union gives the Church its own identity as the Body of Christ.

---

4. Van Bavel, "The 'Christus Totus' Idea," 87–89.

5. "Let us hear them as one single organism, but let us listen to the Head as Head, and the body as body. The persons are not separated, but in dignity they are distinct, for the Head saves and the body is saved." Augustine, *Exp. Ps.* 37.6 (WSA 3/16:151).

6. Augustine, *Exp. Ps.* 30[2].3 (WSA 3/15:322–23).

7. Ibid. (WSA 3/15:323).

8. Ibid.

Augustine, thus, teaches that the Church's identity in Christ begins with Christ's identification with humanity in the Incarnation. While the Incarnation invites all of humanity to share in the life of Christ, he does not impose this relationship. Instead, just as Christ freely identified with humanity, so too is humanity invited to respond freely to Christ and to participate in his life in the Church. Their incorporation into Christ's life takes place in the sacraments that effect an enduring transformation for Christians, giving them a new identity in Christ.

"*You* are the Body of Christ"

For Augustine, the Pauline image of the Church as the Body of Christ is much more than a metaphor; it is a reality. The Church *is* the Body of Christ. Augustine finds the very existence of the Church in the flow of blood and water from Christ's pierced side, the moment that reveals the depths of Christ's solidarity with humanity all the way to death. Just as Eve sprang to life from the side of Adam, so too does Augustine describe the Church springing into life from this flow, interpreted as an image of the sacraments of baptism and the Eucharist.[9] These sacraments bring Christians into union with Christ and continue to nourish the union, thus strengthening their Christian identity, as each generation of Christians is incorporated into the life of Christ.

Augustine's mystagogical preaching to the newly baptized explains the transforming effect of the sacraments. These Christians would have witnessed the sacraments for the first time as they themselves received them, because in Augustine's day those who had not been baptized were dismissed following the Liturgy of the Word. Baptisms would generally take place at the Easter vigil on Holy Saturday, or sometimes on the eve of Pentecost. In his study of the catechumenate in Hippo, William Harmless explains that those to be baptized at Easter had study and preparation all through Lent, a preparation so intense that those who lived in the countryside would actually move into the town for Lent to be closer to the church. Their preparation would include Scripture study, instruction in moral living, fasting, and special rites of exorcism. As Easter drew near, they would be instructed in the Lord's Prayer and then finally be taught the creed orally.[10] All that

---

9. For example, *Exp. Ps.* 40.10, 56.11, 103[4].6, 126.7, 127.11–12, 138.2.

10. Harmless, "Catechumens, Catechumenate," 148. For a more thorough study of the catechumenate, see Harmless, *Augustine and the Catechumenate*.

remained for their study would be the sacraments themselves, so they anticipated the time of mystagogy, or reflection on and explanation of the mysteries, that is, the sacraments, which would extend throughout the octave of Easter.[11] The newly baptized would gather at liturgy each day of Easter week, dressed in their white robes, receiving sacramental formation and instruction before returning to their ordinary lives as changed people. The mystagogical catechesis took place in preaching within the liturgical assembly, thus mature Christians would be reminded of their sacramental transformation in Christ as new Christians heard the instruction for the first time.

Augustine wants the newly baptized to understand that they truly are changed people because of the sacraments. They bear a new reality, a new identity in Christ. In Sermon 229A, preached one year on Easter Sunday, Augustine explains the transformation that the sacraments have effected. He notes the bread and wine on the altar resemble the ordinary bread and wine that could be on the table in their homes, yet in the consecration, the bread and wine of the altar receive a new meaning. So too in baptism, have these Christians received a new meaning:

> What you can see on the Lord's table, as far as the appearance of things goes, you are also used to seeing on your own tables; they have the same aspect, but not the same value. I mean, you yourselves are the same people as you used to be; you haven't brought us along new faces, after all. And yet, you're new; the same old people in bodily appearance, completely new ones by the grace of holiness—just as this too is new.[12]

Not only are the bread and wine transformed into the body and blood of Christ, but the Christians themselves, by virtue of their baptism, now too bear the identity of Christ. Augustine dares to take the words of the apostle Paul in their fullest meaning and see Christians not as reminders of Christ, not so much as "Christ-like," but as Christ himself in the midst of the world long after his historical life on earth has ended.

This identity is held individually and collectively. Each baptized Christian received a "new value" in baptism, and that identity also incorporates

---

11. While today, mystagogy takes place throughout the fifty days of the Easter season extending from Easter to Pentecost, it took place primarily in the eight days of Easter week in Augustine's community. The focus of reflection would be the sacraments of baptism and the Eucharist and their meaning for the lives of Christians.

12. Augustine, *Serm.* 229A.1 (WSA 3/6:269).

them into the community that is Christ. Another Easter Sunday homily makes this point clear. In Sermon 227, Augustine says that he wants to keep the promise made the night before to explain the Eucharist to the newly baptized. He begins with the presence of Christ in the Eucharistic bread and wine themselves: "That bread which you can see on the altar, sanctified by the word of God, is the body of Christ. That cup, or rather what the cup contains, sanctified by the word of God, is the blood of Christ. It was by means of these things that the Lord Christ wished to present us with his body and blood, which he shed for our sake for the forgiveness of sins."[13] Augustine then turns the focus back to the community to find Christ there as well: "If you receive them [the body and blood of Christ] well, you are yourselves what you receive. You see, the apostle says, *We, being many, are one loaf, one body* (1 Cor 10:17). That's how he explained the sacrament of the Lord's table; one loaf, one body, is what we all are, many though we be."[14] In receiving the body and blood of Christ, the Christians themselves are transformed. They become what they receive: Christ.

This transformation brings individual Christians not only into union with Christ, but also with the Church such that together they hold the identity as Christ. The collective identity as Christ gives the Christians a single identity. Rather than many individuals, they now can see themselves as one, a unified whole. Many are made one. Augustine speaks of this transformation of Christians into one body by comparing the initiation process of Christians to the process of forming grains of wheat into a loaf of bread. He says: "In this loaf of bread you are given clearly to understand how much you should love unity. I mean, was that loaf made from one grain? Weren't there many grains of wheat? But before they came into the loaf they were all separate; they were joined together by means of water after a certain amount of pounding and crushing."[15] He then describes the Lenten preparation of fasting and exorcisms as a kind of pounding and crushing followed by a moistening with water. The bread is then ready for baking, just as the Christian would be anointed following baptism, a spiritual "baking" in Augustine's eyes. The Christians are baked into one loaf, the Church, the Body of Christ.

The transformation does not end at Easter. Instead, it is a life-long process of deepening the union with Christ and one another. While the

---

13. Augustine, *Serm.* 227 (WSA 3/6:254).
14. Ibid.
15. Ibid.

sacraments incorporate Christians into the Body of Christ, Augustine teaches Christians to see the entire liturgy as a witness and experience of the *totus Christus*. In his sermons, the liturgy serves as a microcosm of the life of the Body of Christ. He uses the liturgy as instruction on the Incarnation and its effects, forming Christians into the reality of the Body of Christ. Thus, liturgy serves not only as prayer and worship but also as on-going faith formation.

For example, Augustine uses the message of the *totus Christus* to inspire Christians to lift up their hearts:

> First, after the prayer,[16] you are urged to lift up your hearts; that's only right for the members of Christ. After all, if you have become members of Christ, where is your head? . . . What did you give back in the creed? *On the third day he rose again from the dead, he ascended into heaven, he is seated at the right hand of the Father.* So our head is in heaven. That's why, after the words *Lift up your hearts*, you reply, *We have lifted them up to the Lord.*[17]

Augustine's words prepare the Christians to orient themselves toward Christ each time they are called to lift up their hearts.

Similarly, the liturgy can deepen Christian unity, which is essential for receiving the sacrament of the Eucharist. The sign of peace, a holy kiss, exchanged among the assembly expresses the peace that should be in their hearts: "It's a sign of peace; what is indicated by the lips should happen in the conscience; that is, just as your lips approach the lips of your brothers or sisters, so your heart should not be withdrawn from theirs."[18] Augustine does not reduce the unity of Christ to an ideal for which to strive but instead insists it must be present in the community in the here and now, even as the Christians celebrate the liturgy.

The reception of the Eucharist itself, needless to say, has a significant effect on the Church. It has great value, although it is one that may be easy to overlook since the spiritual reality is not visible to the eyes. Augustine explains: "Don't let yourselves think that what you can see is of no account. What you can see passes away, but the invisible reality signified does not pass away, but remains. . . . So receive the sacrament in such a way that you think about yourselves, that you retain unity in your hearts, that you always

---

16. Edmund Hill identifies this prayer as the intercessions of the Prayer of the Faithful that concludes the Liturgy of the Word (WSA 3/6:256n6).

17. Augustine, *Serm.* 227 (WSA 3/6:255).

18. Ibid.

fix your hearts up above."[19] The sacramental transformation endures, not only in the invisible reality of the bread and wine, but also in those who receive it.

Augustine's interpretation of the stages of the liturgy offers Christians a process for on-going reflection on their life as members of Christ's Body. In approaching the rituals as Augustine describes them, the liturgy takes on a formative dimension that deepens the awareness of union with Christ and one another. The process of transformation begun in the sacraments is ongoing as those who entered the Body through baptism continue to be changed through the liturgy and through the Eucharist. Augustine challenges the assembly to understand that they have become members of the Body of Christ and *continue* to grow in the unity of Christ in the celebration of the liturgy. Through the sacraments, Christians have become members of the Body of Christ; that is, members of the *totus Christus*. In the Liturgy, their prayer expresses the union that they have with Christ, and in the Eucharist, they receive the body of Christ that conforms them more fully to Christ. Being a member of the Body of Christ involves a continual transformation as Christians are conformed more and more fully to Christ.

In his mystagogical preaching, Augustine teaches that in baptism, the Christian receives a new identity as Christ. The sacraments bring transformation so that Christ continues to be present in the world in Church. Christian identity is not a static label but rather a life lived with Christ. Specifically, it is a life of loving others with and in Christ because the life of the Church will reflect the life of Christ. Just as it was love that led Christ to the Incarnation in the first place, so too is it love that makes manifest the presence of Christ in the Church. The life of those identified with Christ in the union of the *totus Christus*, then, will be a life marked by love.

Marked by Love

In teaching Christians about their identity in Christ, Augustine teaches them how to live as Christ. Their new identity in Christ leads Christians from the altar back into life in the world. Life with Christ is no private affair but shapes all of one's life, internally and externally. Augustine repeatedly warns Christians not to approach the sacraments as abstracted from their lives and relationships. A powerful example comes in Sermon 260A. In this sermon, Augustine addresses the newly baptized on the octave of their

19. Ibid.

baptism. Throughout the previous week, these new Christians would have sat in a prominent place in the church daily, wearing their white baptismal garments as an external sign of their conversion. Now, eight days into their new life, they were about to set aside the baptismal garments, yet Augustine urges them to continue to have a visible sign of conversion not in clothing but in the way they live their lives.

Augustine begins his sermon with a flurry of Pauline quotations to call the newly baptized to lead lives consistent with the new life they have received in the sacraments. Clothing imagery comes into the homily as he says, "I will address you with the apostle's words," and he quotes the call of Romans 13:13–14, including the call to *"walk honorably, as in the day; not in revelry and drunkenness, not in wanton and shameless behavior, not in rivalry and jealousy; but clothe yourselves with the Lord Jesus Christ."*[20] Augustine then continues with a brief interpretation: "which means, clothe yourselves in your lives with the one you have clothed yourselves with in the sacrament."[21] Even though these Christians would soon set aside their baptismal clothing, their "sacramental clothing" continues to envelop them as they live their lives each day with their new identity as members of the Body of Christ.

Augustine makes clear that the "putting on" of Christ is a sacramental action by using another Pauline passage for support, this time Galatians 3:27–28: *"For as many of you as have been baptized in Christ have put on Christ. . . .* That's done by the very power of the sacrament; it's the sacrament, you see, of the new life."[22] The sacramental union with Christ that gives the Christian a new identity brings with it a new way of living. Christ, the sacraments, and ethics cannot be pulled apart. Augustine says of those who do not live a life consistent with the sacraments: "But there are some people who have put on Christ only in the sacrament, who remain naked in faith or morals."[23] As the newly baptized set aside their garments, Augustine wants them to recognize that their lives will make manifest whether they are clothed spiritually in Christ or left spiritually naked.

20. Augustine, *Serm.* 260A.1 (WSA 3/7:187).

21. Ibid.

22. Ibid.

23. Augustine, *Serm.* 260A.2 (WSA 3/7:188). In the next lines of the sermon, Augustine shows that he has in mind those who break away from the unity of the Church in heresies or schisms: "Even many heretics, I mean, have the actual sacrament of baptism, but not the actual fruit of salvation, nor the bond of peace."

Augustine specifies *caritas*, poured out by the Holy Spirit in baptism, as the prime marker of a transformed life and Christian identity. If one has truly been transformed in Christ, the gift of love will make that conversion manifest. Augustine makes this connection clear in a homily on 1 John: "Love alone, then, distinguishes between children of God and the children of the devil. All may sign themselves with the sign of Christ's cross; all may respond 'Amen'; all may sing 'Alleluia'; all may be baptized; all may go into the churches; all may construct the walls of basilicas. The children of God aren't distinguished from the children of the devil except by charity."[24] Christians are distinguished from others by charity alone, yet Augustine carefully teaches that acts of love are not the achievement of Christians. Rather, Christian love makes manifestation of the gift of love received from the Holy Spirit. When they love, they love in union with Christ. Without love, the sacraments are empty, void of the presence of the Holy Spirit. Love, then, serves as the distinguishing characteristic of Christians, the external marker of their identity in Christ.

Ultimately, *caritas* is the gift of God's very being, thus love is God's presence within the life of a Christian, as Augustine explains in another homily on 1 John: "I don't know whether charity could be commended to us more magnificently than by the words *God is charity* (4:8). . . . *God is love, and he who abides in love*, it says, *abides in God, and God abides in him* (4:16). Let God be your dwelling, and let your dwelling be God's."[25] In Sermon 53A, he describes love as continuing the transformation of the Christian as God dwells in the human heart in love, cleansing it and shaping it from within: "But perhaps you may find difficulty in cleaning out your heart; call him in, he won't refuse to clean out a place for himself, and he will agree to stay with you. . . . I agree, there's nothing greater than God; don't worry, all the same, about not having enough room; receive him, and he enlarges your living space."[26] Love is the shared life of Christians with Christ because love is itself God.

Charity also orients the human heart toward service of neighbor.[27] The same love that drew God into human experience in the Incarnation now graces the lives of Christians and impels them to a life of love in the world.

---

24. Augustine, *Ep. Jo.* 5.7 (WSA 3/14:82). See also, *Ep. Jo.* 6.10; 7.6; 8.1, 12; 10.8.

25. Augustine, *Ep. Jo.* 9.1 (WSA 3/14:132).

26. Augustine, *Serm.* 53A.11 (WSA 3/3:82).

27. A common theme in Augustine's preaching is the two-fold command to love God and neighbor found in Matthew 22:37–40.

God's gift of love motivates and empowers Christians to perform good deeds of love. Charity is the mark of transformation, but without action, love is merely an abstract ideal. To those who claim to love their neighbor, Augustine essentially says, "Prove it." The proof comes in the actions.[28]

Augustine teaches in his sermons that *caritas*, given in the sacraments, takes hold in the life of the Christian and grows as it is put into action. He offers the assembly methods for growing in love. He describes love as beginning with small things, for example, helping someone in need by sharing from one's own abundance. Such kindness is a first step in love. Love, however, is not static but grows with time and experience. Love that reaches maturity reflects Christ's own sacrificial love in that perfect love is the gift of one's very self in laying down one's life for another.[29]

Augustine emphasizes unity as a hallmark of the life of love because unity reflects Christ's own love. The love of the Incarnation is a unitive love that unites God and humanity. Likewise, Christian love unifies. Charity draws Christians not only to God but to others, so human relations reflect the depth of the conversion of heart. Unity is a sign of the presence of love, and thus the presence of Christ.

The starting point for unity among people is the Church, the Body of Christ. Having entered the union of the *totus Christus*, the whole Christ, Christians find themselves united to all Christians in the one Body of Christ. The Christian life is one led in common with the entire community of faith. He explains that charity leads Christians to bear with the shortcomings of one another in the bonds of the Church. Thus, Church unity is a prime sign of love in the world. More than a failure of doctrine, Augustine considers Church schism to be a failure to love.[30]

The unifying effects of charity lead the Church also to reach out to others in the works of mercy. Augustine insists that Christ is present in all human need, thus calling Christians to recognize Christ in those who suffer. Matthew 25:31–40 provides him with support for this claim. To those who lament that they do not have the opportunity to encounter Christ personally as those in biblical times did, Augustine issues a challenge to see Christ in those in need: "Don't be disappointed, don't grumble because you

---

28. Augustine preaches, "If action comes with the name, show that you are a Christian by your deeds." *Ep. Jo.* 5.12 (WSA 3/14:86).

29. While acknowledging that not everyone will reach such a mature stage of love, Augustine encourages Christians to nurture love in their lives so that it will grow. *Ep. Jo.* 5.11–12; 6.1.

30. Augustine, *Ep. Jo.* 10.8.

were born at a time when you could not now see the Lord in the flesh. He hasn't, in fact, deprived you of this privilege and honor: *when you did it*, he says, *to one of the least of mine, you did it to me* (Mt 25:40)."[31] Christ's loving unity with humanity includes those in need, thus Christian love brings the Church also into solidarity with them. Such solidarity includes concrete efforts to alleviate human need and suffering. Because of Christ's enduring union with needy humanity, the Church serves Christ by serving others in concrete acts of love.[32]

Love also moves Christians to seek reconciliation with those whom they find the most difficult to love. Augustine recognizes the challenges of loving one's enemy. He does not expect the Christian suddenly to drop all ill feeling but instead says that charity begins by moving the Christian to long for the good of one's enemy, a simple yet essential starting point. With time, one comes to pray the enemy back into fellowship, whether on a personal or community level. Perhaps such efforts of reconciliation are the true test of charity. Charity demands that the Christian come to accept being united with people who are annoying, offensive, and needless to say, sinful.[33]

The *caritas* that marks the Christian life draws Christians into Christ's own life by leading them to act as Christ in the world. Their identity in Christ comes alive as they live as Christ lived. Acts of love strive for unity within Christ's Body, alleviation of human suffering, and reconciliation of enemies, thus reflecting Christ's own unifying love in the Incarnation. As they grow in such love, Christians radiate Christ's own love such that others recognize Christ in their life in the world.

Seeing Christ in the Church

Christians may be called to make Christ manifest to the world, but Augustine acknowledges that the real challenge can be for them even to recognize Christ among themselves. He teaches frequently about love and unity because the Church lacked the very unity that he says is Christ's. His own North

---

31. Augustine, *Serm.* 103.2 (WSA 3/4:77).

32. Augustine's insistence that Christ continues to be present in needy humanity lends some ambiguity in his doctrine of the *totus Christus*. At times, he specifies that Christ is present in needy Christians, while at other times he seems to suggest that Christ is present in needy humanity as a whole. In *Serm.* 38.8, for example, Augustine explicitly identifies Christ with all people who are poor.

33. See, for example, *Ep. Jo.* 1.9–11; 8.4, 10; 10.7.

African Church had been split apart during the Donatist crisis.[34] In fact, Augustine sharpened his doctrine of the *totus Christus* in this context of Church schism. His doctrine is not an abstract ideal but a call to seek unity in the face of division. As he shapes their sacramental vision, Augustine continually instructs Christians that they hold in common their identity in Christ, thus they should recognize not only themselves as identified with Christ, but their fellow Christians as members of the one Body of Christ.

Augustine saw the heart of the schism to be a failure to recognize Christ in other Christians. He acknowledges common ground with the Donatists, deeming their theology as orthodox with the only exception coming from their schism with the Catholics. That schism is no small difference in Augustine's mind, though. Because Christ and the Church share an identity in the unbreakable bond of the *totus Christus*, schism is a failure to love not only fellow Christians but Christ himself. Preaching on 1 John, he proclaims: "Spread your charity throughout the world, if you want to love Christ, because Christ's members lie throughout the world. If you love a section, you have been cut off; if you have been cut off, you aren't in the body; if you aren't in the body, you aren't under the head."[35] Christ and the Church share an identity that runs so deep that Augustine can say to love Christ, love your fellow Christian.

So too Augustine says if you want to see Christ, look to the Church. Augustine admits that this is easier said than done, because to see Christ in the Church requires the eyes of faith. For this reason, he suggests that the

---

34. The crisis dates back to the aftermath of the severe persecution of Christians throughout the Roman Empire in 303–304. One of the consecrators of the new bishop installed in Carthage soon afterward was alleged to have betrayed the faith by handing over sacred books to the persecutors. Although the charges were determined to be unfounded, many Christians split from communion with that bishop and chose their own bishop in Carthage. The Christians who joined in this division were known as "Donatists." The schism spread quickly throughout North Africa, and often had a violent edge to it leading to martyrs for both sides. By the time Augustine was ordained, the Donatists greatly outnumbered the Catholics in Hippo. Much of his first two decades of ordained ministry were marked by his efforts to reunite the churches. For a brief introduction to the Donatist controversy, see Markus, "Donatus, Donatism," 284–87.

35. Augustine, *Ep. Jo.* 10.8 (WSA 3/14:155). Augustine goes so far as to say that to break unity with the Church is to deny that Christ has come in the flesh, to deny the union of Christ with the Church: "I find that Christ is the bridegroom of the Church spread throughout the whole wide world. If you say he is the other thing [the bridegroom of the Donatists], and he isn't the other thing [the bridegroom of the Catholics], then you are denying that Christ has come in the flesh." Augustine, *Serm.* 183.11 (WSA 3/5:341–42).

biblical writers actually spent more time writing about the Church than about Christ, because even those who can find agreement in Christ would struggle with belief in the Church: "Yet the prophets spoke more clearly about the Church than about Christ, because, I think, they saw in spirit that it was in opposition to the Church that people would found their conventicles. They would not engage in such intense argument about Christ himself; it would be about the Church that they would raise the fiercest quarrels."[36] Augustine too spent a vast amount of time and energy preaching on the *totus Christus* and working for Church unity. His efforts reflect the difficulty of truly honoring Christ in the Church throughout the world. One can affirm Christ in words easier than in deeds.[37]

Augustine may put the focus on the struggle to understand the Church, but ultimately for him this struggle points back to Christ because the Church's identity lies in Christ. The challenge is to recognize Christ present in the Church, the entire Church. To see Christ in the Church means to recognize the identity held in common by all Christians, including those who may be more difficult to love. It requires a sacramental vision because it is a matter of learning to recognize the invisible, spiritual realities present in the visible realities.

Augustine says that the challenge Christians face of recognizing Christ made manifest in the Church is a shift from the one the disciples would have faced. The disciples could see Christ with their eyes; he was physically present to them. The challenge for them would have been to envision the Church still yet to come. On this side of Christ's ascension, though, the situation has been reversed. Christians now can see the Church visibly before them. It is Christ who is not visibly present before them. During the Easter Octave, he preached:

> We can't see Christ, we can see this Church; about him we have to believe. The apostles, on the contrary, could see him, could only believe about this Church. They could see one thing, believe the other; and we on the contrary can see one thing, must believe the other. They could see Christ, could only believe about the Church, which they couldn't see. We too can see the Church, must believe in Christ, whom we cannot see.[38]

---

36. Augustine, *Exp. Ps.* 30[3].8 (WSA 3/15:341).

37. In one sermon, Augustine says, "What is denying by your deeds? Being proud and making schisms; making your boast not in God, but in man. That's how Christ is denied by deeds; Christ, of course, loves unity." *Serm.* 183.10 (WSA 3/5:340).

38. Augustine, *Serm.* 238.3 (WSA 3/7:58).

He concludes the sermon saying that through the Church, one will discover Christ: "By holding on to what we can see, we shall finally reach him whom we cannot yet see."[39] The visible Church, then, leads to Christ, who is invisible in the present. The Church leads to Christ because the Church *is* Christ, bears the identity of Christ in the world, thus one encounters Christ in the present in the Church.

This conviction that the Church makes manifest the presence of Christ resonates with Augustine's sacramental theology. He defines a sacrament as a visible sign of an invisible reality. For example, when explaining the sacrament of the Eucharist to new Christians, he says: "The reason these things, brothers and sisters, are called sacraments is that in them one thing is seen, another is to be understood. What can be seen has a bodily appearance, what is to be understood provides spiritual fruit."[40] The sacrament mediates a spiritual and transformative reality. In the case of the Eucharist, Augustine explains that what is seen is the visible bread and wine; when blessed they express or mediate what is not visible: the presence of Christ. By virtue of their baptism and reception of the Eucharist, he tells the new Christians that they now bear a new reality as well: a new identity as members of the Body of Christ.[41]

In the same way, the visible Church as a whole makes manifest an invisible, spiritual reality: the presence of Christ. Human failings do not necessarily diminish the Church's identity in Christ. In spite of human weakness, the Church bears Christ's presence because Christ has chosen to live in union with the Church in love and thus empower the Church to live as Christ. It is Christ's choice to identify with sinful humanity that preserves the Church's identity in Christ. Even in the face of ecclesial divisions and shortcomings, Augustine trusts in the concrete presence of Christ in the life of the Church as strongly as he believes in the concrete presence of Christ in the sacrament of the Eucharist. The Church bears the identity of Christ because it bears the presence of Christ in the world.

Preaching as Mystagogical Catechesis

Augustine's doctrine of the *totus Christus* serves as a statement of faith in the sacramental presence of Christ in the Church that holds together

---

39. Ibid.
40. Augustine, *Serm.* 272 (WSA 3/7:300).
41. Ibid.

Christ, sacrament, and the Church in a unified whole, in the one identity of Christ. His preaching on the doctrine has a mystagogical dimension that instructs Christians on who they have become in the sacraments and how they are to live in this new reality. When Augustine tells new Christians: "*You, though, are the body of Christ and its members*. . . . it's the mystery meaning you,"[42] he forms them in their sacramental identity as Christ; a mystery to be sure, but a reality, not a metaphor.

This message reaches beyond the new Christians, however, to Augustine's North African community more broadly. He does not limit the mystagogical catechesis to the newly baptized, but instead offers the explanation of the sacraments in the midst of the full liturgical assembly. Thus new Christians and experienced Christians receive this instruction together each year during Easter week. As such, the Christian community experiences mystagogical formation each year at Easter, deepening and renewing its understanding of the sacraments and its identity in Christ.

One could say that Augustine's preaching on the doctrine of the *totus Christus* itself, regardless of its liturgical time and place, serves as a form of mystagogical catechesis as it explains the sacramental reality of the Church as the Body of Christ and sharpens the sacramental awareness of Christians so that they see Christ more clearly in the Church and throughout the world. During Easter week, his mystagogical preaching on baptism and the Eucharist ultimately is formation in the doctrine of *totus Christus* and the identity that Christians receive in Christ. Likewise, throughout the year, when he preaches on the *totus Christus*, he instructs the community on the sacramental unity of the Church and Christ, heightening Christians' understanding of Christ's presence in and among them.

Augustine's preaching serves as a primary means of faith formation and religious education for his community in Hippo. His instruction offers Christians more than information about the faith but seeks to form them in their identity and relationship with Christ such that their lives express the faith they profess as they live and love with Christ. In this way, his preaching of the doctrine of the *totus Christus* does what Michael Connors has said that "great Christian preaching of every age seeks to do." It seeks not "purely intellectual instruction but *metanoia*, conversion of the whole person to Christ."[43]

---

42. Ibid.
43. Connors, "A Living Word of Hope for the Whatever Generation," 234.

For Augustine, this conversion is individual and corporate as Christians together grow in their identity and life in Christ. The same sacramental vision that leads Christians to find Christ at the altar also leads them to see Christ in themselves and the Church community and to act as Christ in the world through acts of love. Christ may not be visibly present before them, but Christ lives among them and in them, now made manifest in their very lives. In the union of the *totus Christus*, they have become one with Christ and one another. Thus, Augustine can say with confidence, "What you receive [the body of Christ] is what you yourselves are, thanks to the grace by which you have been redeemed."[44]

List of Abbreviations

Ep. Jo.   *Homilies on the First Epistle of John*
Exp. Ps.   *Expositions of the Psalms*
Serm.   *Sermons*
WSA   The Works of Saint Augustine: A Translation for the 21st Century

Bibliography

Augustine. *Expositions of the Psalms*. Translated by Maria Boulding. Edited by John Rotelle. The Works of Saint Augustine: A Translation for the 21st Century 3/15–20. Hyde Park, NY: New City, 2000–2004.

———. *Homilies on the First Epistle of John*. Translated by Boniface Ramsey. Edited by Daniel E. Doyle and Thomas Martin. The Works of Saint Augustine: A Translation for the 21st Century 3/14. Hyde Park, NY: New City, 2008.

———. *Sermons*. Translated by Edmund Hill. Edited by John E. Rotelle. The Works of Saint Augustine: A Translation for the 21st Century 3/1–11. Hyde Park, NY: New City, 1993–97.

Connors, Michael E. "A Living Word of Hope for the Whatever Generation." In *We Preach Christ Crucified*, edited by Michael E. Connors, 227–37. Collegeville, MN: Liturgical, 2014.

Harmless, William. *Augustine and the Catechumenate*, rev. ed. Collegeville, MN: Liturgical, 2014.

———. "Catechumens, Catechumenate." In *Augustine Through the Ages: An Encyclopedia*, edited by Allan D. Fitzgerald, 145–49. Grand Rapids, MI: Eerdmans, 1999.

Markus, Robert A. "Donatus, Donatism." In *Augustine through the Ages: An Encyclopedia*, edited by Allan D. Fitzgerald, 284–87. Grand Rapids, MI: Eerdmans, 1999.

Tyconius. *The Book of Rules*. Edited and translated by William S. Babcock. Atlanta, GA: Scholars, 1989.

---

44. Augustine, *Serm.* 229A.1 (WSA 3/6:270).

Van Bavel, Tarsicius. "The 'Christus Totus' Idea: A Forgotten Aspect of Augustine's Spirituality." In *Studies in Patristic Christology: Proceedings of the Third Maynooth Patristic Conference*, edited by Thomas Finan and Vincent Twomey, 84–94. Portland, OR: Four Courts, 1998.

3

Catholic Identity and Religious Education in Modern Poland

—Robert E. Alvis

Introduction

ONE OF THE HALLMARKS of modernity is the principle of educating all children in a given society from childhood to young adulthood. Universal education of this sort entails the creation of elaborate systems designed to impart general knowledge, including literacy and numeracy, that can serve as a foundation for the subsequent acquisition of more specialized expertise. This model stands in sharp contrast to premodern educational models, which were more modest and diffuse. Historically, it was the privileged few who benefited from formal education stretching over many years. The large majority received little or no formal education outside of the home or within the context of a specific profession.

Various observers have drawn a connection between the rise of universal education and the changing nature of work in a world transformed by industrialization. As Ernest Gellner notes, "Universal literacy and a high level of numerical, technical and general sophistication are among [industrial society's] functional prerequisites. Its members are and must be mobile, and ready to shift from one activity to another, and must possess that generic training which enables them to follow manuals and instructions of a new activity and occupation. In the course of their work they must constantly communicate with a large number of other men, with whom they frequently have no previous association."[1]

Another distinctive feature of modern education is the prominent role of the state in determining its content and orchestrating its delivery. In the West, the state gradually crowded out religious organizations, the traditional purveyors of education. Driving this development was the recognition of education's potential to shape the identities and values of young people in ways that could strengthen social cohesion and enhance the legitimacy of the state. "At the base of the modern social order stands not the executioner but the professor," Gellner observes. "The monopoly of legitimate education is now more important, more central than the monopoly of legitimate violence."[2]

For many in the Roman Catholic Church, the gradual unfolding of this novel educational paradigm, like so many other facets of modernity, has been deeply troubling, and they have fought hard to defend the church's traditional vision of education. The purpose of education, in this view, is the cultivation of knowledge *and* faith, forming people who can contribute to the common good within a proper moral framework and with an eye toward the ultimate goal of salvation. The church itself should be the arbiter of the religious dimension of education. An educational system that dispenses practical knowledge devoid of a transcendent referent represents an abdication of society's obligation to its children.

One of the most high-profile defenses of the Catholic vision of education can be found in Pope Pius XI's 1929 encyclical *Divini illius magistri*. At the heart of his argument are the rights of Christian children: "Every Christian child or youth has a strict right to instruction in harmony with the teaching of the Church, the pillar and ground of truth. And whoever disturbs the pupil's faith in any way, does him grave wrong." The demands of contemporary society require a model of education that exceeds the capacity of most families, the pope concedes, so formal schools are necessary. As it approaches the work of such schools, however, the state should defer to the rights of the family and the church. The school "owes its existence to the initiative of the family and of the Church, long before it was undertaken by the state. Hence, considered in its historical origin, the school is by its very nature an institution subsidiary and complementary to the family and the Church." The mere inclusion of religion as one subject within a curriculum

---

1. Gellner, *Nations and Nationalism*, 35.
2. Ibid., 34.

that is otherwise uninformed by Christian perspectives is insufficient, the pope argues. Ideally, a school's teachers, curriculum, and textbooks should be "regulated by the Christian spirit, under the direction and maternal supervision of the Church; so that religion may be in very truth the foundation and crown of the youth's entire training." The purely secular school, the pope warns, is "contrary to the fundamental principles of education."[3]

This chapter examines the Catholic Church's struggle to defend what it regarded as its rights and obligations regarding primary and secondary education in the context of modern Poland. The analysis is broken down into four phases. The first is the partition era (1772–1918), when the neighboring countries of Prussia, Russia, and Austria divided Poland's territory among themselves and Poland essentially ceased to exist. Educational systems developed in distinctive ways in each of the partitions; for the sake of simplicity, this chapter focuses only on the Prussian (and later German) partition. The second phase is the interwar era (1918–1939), when Poland reemerged as an independent country. The third phase is the communist era (1945–1989), a time when Polish affairs were shaped profoundly by the priorities of the Soviet Union. The fourth and final phase is the postcommunist era (1989 to the present).

Over the course of these four phases, the Catholic Church's ability to achieve its educational priorities varied widely. I argue that the degree to which the church was successful in defining formal education did not always correspond to the degree to which it was able to shape the identities and values of young Catholics. Ironically, in periods when hostile governments excluded the church from the educational arena, lay Catholics tended to embrace their religion more tightly and find alternative means to expose their children to its teachings. Conversely, in periods when the church's influence over education grew more pronounced, the institution could be perceived by Catholics and non-Catholics alike as overly domineering, which could suppress Catholic enthusiasm for their faith. Behind this dynamic is another signal feature of modernity: the high esteem for human autonomy, especially in matters of conscience. Catholic leaders violated this principle at their own risk.

---

3. Ulich, *A History of Religious Education*, 259–63.

Partition-Era Prussia and Germany

A series of disasters befell the Commonwealth of Poland and Lithuania over the second half of the seventeenth and early years of the eighteenth centuries, reducing this once powerful state to a shell of its former self. Its weakness tempted Prussia, Russia, and Austria to divide its territory among themselves in 1772, 1793, and finally in 1795, when the commonwealth disappeared from the map. The Polish people lived under Prussian (German), Russian, and Austrian rule for the next 123 years.

The partition era coincided with the development of an increasingly comprehensive system of education for children and young adults living in Polish regions. As this took place, the partitioning powers generally were keen to ensure that the educational process would promote loyalty to the ruling state and affection for its predominant culture. These efforts were countered by the emergence of an increasingly sophisticated Polish nationalist movement determined to promote Polish identity, in part through education, with the ultimate goal of reestablishing an independent Polish state.

In the Polish lands claimed by Prussia, the struggle over national identity became entangled with a contest between the state and the Catholic Church over education. Catholic leaders championed the causes of religious instruction and church oversight in the educational arena. Prussian officials, while predominantly Protestant, were not necessarily opposed to this. In the nineteenth century, religious instruction was widely regarded as integral to the formation of disciplined, law-abiding citizens. In general, however, the state claimed an increasingly dominant role over the school system. Adding urgency to this drive was the growing recognition that Catholic religious instruction was dovetailing with the push to promote Polish national identity. This motivated the state to tighten its grip on education, sometimes embracing extreme measures that had the unintended consequences of strengthening the church's hand.

Prussian educational policy in its Polish territories passed through a number of distinct phases. The first phase ran from the start of the partition era in 1772 to 1806, when Prussian control was disrupted by Napoleon. At this time, Prussia was an early leader in the drive to establish a comprehensive system of education. It regarded the educational system in its newly acquired Polish lands to be deficient in several respects: too few children were enrolled, Polish language and culture were too prominent, and the Catholic Church had too much control. Prussian officials recognized the potential of education to modernize the Polish territories and promote assimilation into Prussian culture. While some progress was made in terms of expanding the educational infrastructure, training teachers, and bolstering the obligation of children to attend, these efforts were hampered by the state's parsimony. One feature left undisturbed was the Catholic Church's control over schools designated for Catholic children, even though many Prussian officials regarded the church as hopelessly backward. This sentiment is captured in the lament of Karl Georg von Hoym, a high-ranking official in Silesia, to his colleague Otto von Voss in 1793: "All my simple efforts to make of the Polish Upper Silesian clergy, schoolmasters, and children German-mannered people and to introduce new methods of instruction have been frustrated by the upper clergy, who worked so long against them that I lost my determination and strength." What redeemed the church in the government's eyes was its conservativism, which helped guard the educational arena from "so-called Enlighteners who inspire democratic principles" in students.[4]

After helping drive Napoleon from the region, Prussia reasserted its control over Polish territory in 1815. Cognizant of how Polish patriotic fervor had been enflamed during the Napoleonic era, over the next fifteen years Prussia ruled with a conciliatory spirit, hoping to win the hearts and minds of Poles by respecting their culture and predominant religion. This same ethos informed educational policy.[5] Prussia made major investments in education at this time, expanding the network of schools and cadre of teachers and raising enrollment rates. Enrollment continued to take place along confessional lines, and the state did not challenge the Catholic Church's supervision of Catholic schools and the provision of religious education. Polish remained the primary language of instruction for Polish youth, with the exception of the higher grades in *Gymnasium*, where German-language instruction was designed to prepare students interested in attending German universities. Karl vom Stein zum Altenstein, a leading architect of Prussian education policy in these years, encapsulated the hopes of this period well when he noted: "Religion and mother tongue are the most sacred possessions of a nation. In them its whole mentality and style of thought are grounded. The government which recognizes, respects, and protects them may be sure of winning the hearts of its subjects; but a

---

4. Hagan, *Germans, Poles, and Jews*, 58.

5. For detailed treatment of education in the Poznań region in the nineteenth and early twentieth centuries, see Truchim, *Historia szkolnictwa i oświaty*.

government which shows itself indifferent to them, or even allows attacks upon them, embitters and dishonors a nation and makes of its members untrue and bad subjects."[6]

This conciliatory approach yielded mixed results. Prussia's Polish territories remained peaceful, and numerous Polish conservative elites cooperated closely with the state, but Prussian police also uncovered evidence of conspiratorial activity by Polish nationalist activists. Prussian fears were magnified further still when hundreds of Prussian Poles crossed into Russia to support a Polish uprising there in 1830–31. These developments prompted Prussia to adopt a much harder line toward the culture of its Polish subjects. The man charged with introducing this policy in the Grand Duchy of Poznań, the Prussian region with the greatest concentration of Poles, was Eduard Flottwell. He summarized the goals of his tenure as follows: "To strengthen [the province's] ties to the Prussian state, whereby the efforts, habits, and tendencies of the Polish inhabitants to resist such ties are gradually eliminated and the German element in its material and intellectual dimension is increasingly extended, until which point the goal of complete union of both nationalities through the dominance of German culture is achieved."[7] In the sphere of education, Flottwell gave greater scope to German-language instruction and sought to increase the enrollment and quality of schools not under the control of the Catholic Church.

Growing numbers of Poles, including many members of the clergy, came to regard Prussia's more repressive approach as an attack on their culture and religion. As tensions rose, a new king, Friedrich Wilhelm IV, assumed the Prussian throne in 1840. He promptly called for a milder course toward his Polish subjects, which resulted in a number of changes in educational policy. A new school ordinance enacted in 1842 reaffirmed the principle of education in one's mother tongue through the early years of *Gymnasium*. For native Polish speakers, during the higher years of *Gymnasium* subjects were to be taught in German, except for religion, Polish history, and Polish literature. A Catholic section was established within the Ministry of Education, and its officials were expected to work with local clergy affiliated with the Archdiocese of Gniezno-Poznań in supervising schools designated for Catholic children. Prussia's Polish population generally welcomed these changes, but it did not lead to a cessation of Polish conspiratorial activity. One source of consternation was the Catholic

---

6. Hagan, *Germans, Poles, and Jews*, 82.
7. Alvis, *Religion and the Rise of Nationalism*, 51.

Gymnasium in Poznań, where its director, Fr. Jakub Prabucki, and four Polish teachers were fired in 1846 for fomenting dissent. A year later, Fr. Aleksy Prusinowski was dismissed for what government officials regarded as subversive pedagogy.[8]

A major test of Prussia's success at winning over its Polish subjects came in the Springtime of Nations in 1848, when popular revolutions erupted in many corners of Europe, including in Berlin, where the king temporarily lost his grip on the reins of power. Nationalist Poles in the Grand Duchy of Poznań commandeered key centers of power in the province and launched a bid for independence. Their gambit enjoyed considerable support within the Polish population, including the Catholic clergy, before the Prussian army suppressed it. The disturbance killed any lingering illusions that the Poles could be won over by respecting their culture and dominant religion. Thereafter, the government pursued a more aggressive course, varying only in intensity, up to the outbreak of World War I. Education policy figured prominently in this campaign, though not initially. During the 1850s and 1860s, the school ordinance of 1842 remained largely in effect, and local clergy continued to supervise Catholic schools. Prussian officials promoted the expansion and quality of German-language schools and steered more students there.

The creation of the German Empire in 1871 led to marked shifts in educational policy that were embedded in larger political strategies, including an acute anti-Catholicism and an accelerated Germanization effort in the Prussian East. Germany's chancellor in these years, Otto von Bismarck, seeking to attract the political support of liberals who despised the Catholic Church as hopelessly antithetical to progress, launched a multipronged campaign against the church's influence and autonomy that has come to be known as the *Kulturkampf*. Clergy who resisted risked deportation or imprisonment. The campaign was especially pronounced in Polish regions, where Catholicism was recognized as nurturing Polish separatism. These initiatives had significant implications for education. Early developments included the elimination of the Catholic section of the Ministry of Education, and the replacement of clergy with lay people in the supervision of Catholic schools. Decrees in 1873–74 named German as the official language of instruction in all elementary and secondary schools in the Poznań Province. Henceforth, Polish was to be used only as an aid in helping students master German and for the teaching of religion to Polish Catholic students.

8. Ibid., 72.

The anti-Catholic, anti-Polish initiatives emanating out of Berlin outraged Polish Catholics, further deepening the sense of estrangement from the national government. It also sparked various forms of organized resistance. In the field of education, the dismantling of Polish-language instruction that honored Polish culture inspired private initiatives designed to rectify the loss. This included the expansion of an impressive system of private lending libraries that could supply Polish families with Polish literature. By 1890, nearly a thousand such libraries existed, circulating tens of thousands of books. Members of the Catholic clergy worked closely with the Polish gentry and intelligentsia to facilitate this work.[9]

It eventually became evident that the *Kulturkampf* was doing more political harm than good, particularly by uniting Catholics into a potent force that could sway elections. Bismarck began to soften his stance toward the church in 1878, though aspects of the *Kulturkampf* remained in effect well into the 1880s. After Bismarck fell from power in 1890, his successor, Leo von Caprivi, aiming to win the support of Polish representatives in parliament, introduced a modest liberalization of education policy in Polish regions. This included the expansion of Polish-language instruction, including in the study of religion.

This period of liberalization collapsed with Caprivi's government in 1894, giving way to a more repressive phase lasting to 1914. A directive in 1900 called for German to be introduced as the language of instruction in religion classes throughout the Polish territories. This change inspired the phenomenon of school strikes, starting in the town of Września and spreading elsewhere. Polish Catholic children, with the support and encouragement of their parents, began refusing to attend German-language religion classes. The harsh reprisals of school and state officials, including brutal forms of corporal punishment and the prosecution of parents who rose to their children's defense, greatly magnified the impact of the strikes. Officials eventually managed to break the first strikes, but subsequent strikes erupted over the next several years, and the issue inspired a new wave of organizing by Polish Catholics, including the creation of a petition against German-language religion instruction that attracted some 150,000 signatures. Polish Catholic clerics responded to the state's latest challenge by lengthening the time children spent in sacramental training outside of school, which enhanced the clergy's ability to form the identities and

---

9. Hagan, *Germans, Poles, and Jews*, 141–42.

values of their charges.[10] As with earlier instances of repressive policies, the state's hard line on religious education was generally counterproductive. As Hagan observes, "The government's exclusion of Polish language instruction from the public school curriculum merely heightened the Poles' sense of discrimination at German hands while strengthening their attachment to those Polish institutions—church, nationalist cultural societies, press—which assumed the schools' job of teaching and cultivating their mother-tongue."[11]

The Second Polish Republic

The Great War pitted the partitioning powers against one another, which helped create an opening for Polish independence by war's end. Polish leaders cobbled together territories previously ruled by Germany, Russia, and Austria into what has come to be known as the Second Polish Republic.

The Catholic Church in Poland entered this new era shaped profoundly by the repressive policies experienced under German and Russian rule. Finding themselves in a more favorable climate, church leaders were determined to put a Catholic stamp on the new country, including its educational policies. While Catholics constituted a solid majority of the republic's population, around 36 percent of its inhabitants belonged to other religions or no religion at all, and this non-Catholic population had little interest in living in an explicitly Catholic country. Catholic leaders had the means to achieve many of their objectives, but the harder they pushed, the more they united religious minorities and the non-religious in opposition. This heightened inter-religious tensions and generated considerable resentment among Catholic leaders toward religious minorities.

As the republic's leaders set about building a system of universal education for children and young adults, a return to the wide ranging control the church once enjoyed, and which Pope Pius XI identified as ideal in his 1929 encyclical, simply was not tenable. Even though the church could claim a healthy majority of the population, it lacked the clout to bring this more traditional vision of education into effect.[12] By the 1920s, a modern vision of education as the proper responsibility of government had set down deep

10. See Korth, *Die preussische Schulpolitik*.

11. Hagan, *Germans, Poles, and Jews*, 296.

12. For insight into the interwar Polish Catholic view on education, see Adamski, *Szkoła wedle nauki Kościoła*.

roots in Poland. In this view, education should prepare new generations to contribute to a thriving industrial economy and inculcate the patriotism and civic virtues that could sustain a unified, healthy society. One of the early legislative achievements of the newly formed interwar government was a law requiring all youth to attend school for seven years. In subsequent years, the government established a system of educational tracks to accommodate a range of vocational aspirations. The core curriculum that emerged emphasized love of and service to the Second Republic.

Catholic leaders proved quick studies of the specific features of Poland's new parliamentary democracy, which enabled them to achieve some of their top legislative priorities. They were successful in shielding church property from the process of land reform being advanced by parties appealing to the peasantry. Church leaders also managed to shape the content of the March Constitution of 1921. That document did not identify Catholicism as the republic's official religion—something the church eagerly sought—but Article 114 listed Catholicism as the first among the religions officially recognized by the state. Furthermore, Catholicism was the only religion guaranteed the right to "govern itself by its own laws." Article 120 established mandatory religious education in public schools, another church desideratum. As this law came into effect, the church enjoyed largely unfettered control over the curriculum and the personnel employed to teach religion to Catholic children.

Another church triumph was the 1925 concordat struck between Poland and the Vatican, which yielded a new set of rights that other religious communities did not enjoy. The concordat guaranteed Catholics religious freedom and unrestricted communication with the Vatican. It granted the papacy the right to appoint Catholic bishops in Polish dioceses, with the Polish president holding the right to veto papal appointments. Clergy accused of crimes could now look forward to being judged by their peers in church courts rather than in the republic's judicial system. In the sphere of education, the state agreed to subsidize the salaries and pensions of those providing religious instruction in the nation's schools.[13]

While the Catholic Church did not gain the kind of comprehensive oversight of the education of Catholic children that it once exercised, it was able to ensure that religious instruction was a required component of education, to choose the instructors tasked with this work, to control the

---

13. For detailed treatment of the church's role in education in the interwar era, see Szczepaniak, *Troska Kościoła o nauczanie*, and Szczepaniak, *Episkopat w obronie*.

curriculum Catholic students encountered, and to secure state financing for this work. It is reasonable to assume that this system promoted Catholic identity and the internalization of Catholic values among the students who experienced it, though it would be difficult to find concrete data to support this assertion. The church no longer had to contend with overtly hostile governments, but this was perhaps as much of a blessing as it was a curse. In the partition era, heavy-handed state repression tended to rally Catholics in defense of their faith and inspired a range of creative educational initiatives.

Catholic achievements in the sphere of education were one aspect of a larger political program that generated significant costs. The church used its demographic weight to carve out a privileged position in Polish society, but this inspired a sense of grievance among other religious groups. It also alienated liberals, who regarded the outsized role the church claimed for itself as a violation of religion's proper place in a liberal democracy. It certainly did not help that many Catholic priests and prelates were unabashed in demonstrating their support for right-wing political parties. Polish Catholics thus had to wrestle with the resentment of non-Catholics and the common accusation that the church was out of step with the times and an impediment to progress.

There is evidence to suggest that the church's larger political program alienated some Poles from the Catholic faith. One can point, for instance, to Henryk Dembiński (1908–1941), who as a young man rose to a position of prominence in the Catholic student group "Rebirth" at the University of Vilnius, before cutting his ties with the church and affiliating with the Polish Socialist Party. Dembiński never ceased being a Christian, but he ultimately found it impossible to reconcile his progressive political leanings with the church of his day.[14] Another example is the writer, actor, and activist Jerzy Zawieyski (1902–1969), who abandoned atheism for Catholicism in the 1930s, but not without considerable struggle. Like Dembiński he was a political progressive, and the illiberal tenor of interwar Catholicism repelled him. "What did Catholicism and the Church mean for us, former socialists and believers, in the 1920s? I must painfully admit that the Church itself, in the person of its officials and its clergy, constituted for us the greatest obstacle on the road to Catholicism and faith. Catholicism seemed to us to be identical with anti-Semitism, fascism, obscurantism, fanaticism, and all that was antiprogressive and anticultural."[15]

14. Michnik, *The Church and the Left*, 36–37.
15. Ibid., 34–35.

Poland under Communism

The Second Polish Republic collapsed under the impact of the German and Soviet invasions in 1939, and for the next six years Poles had to contend with a harsh occupation that decimated the population and wreaked havoc with its economy and culture. Formal education evaporated under a new regime that viewed much of the prewar Polish population as fit for little more than slave labor. An independent Poland reemerged after Germany's defeat in 1945, and among the pressing issues its government faced was the challenge of recreating a system of universal education. The essential resources were all in short supply, as were the funds to pay for them. The earliest postwar curricula showed much continuity with the interwar era, including a place for religious education.

The Soviet Union, which "liberated" Poland by driving out the German occupier, was determined to keep the country in its sphere of influence. Toward that end, it shepherded the rise of the communist Polish United Workers' Party (Polska Zjednoczona Partia Robotnicza, PZPR). As it consolidated its authority over the country, the PZPR proceeded cautiously with the Catholic Church, recognizing that the church's popularity and moral authority greatly exceeded its own. Although ideologically opposed to religion, communist leaders allowed religious instruction to continue being offered in public schools and for priests and religious to serve as instructors. At the same time, it began shaping the curriculum according to its own priorities, introducing a place for Marxist-Leninist thought, Russian language instruction, and a socialist reading of Poland's history and current geopolitical alignment.[16]

In 1948, Stalinist hardliner Bolesław Bierut displaced the more moderate Władysław Gomułka as head of the PZPR, and he initiated a more aggressive stance toward the church, seeking to strip it of its outsized role in public affairs and to sow mistrust of church leaders among Poles. The church absorbed a series of blows, including the banning of most lay Catholic associations, its exclusion from engagement in the field of health care and charitable assistance, and the nationalization of most church property outside of worship spaces and residences. Keen to limit the damage, Poland's bishops signed a controversial agreement with the state in 1950. In exchange for honoring the authority of the communist regime, supporting its priorities in negotiations with the Vatican, and opposing the last vestiges

---

16. Janowski, "Polish Education," 41–46.

of underground resistance to communist control, the bishops won a number of concessions, including the survival of religious education in schools. Their hopes for more stable church-state relations dissipated, however, as the regime intensified its assault over the next six years. One of its targets was religious education. It shuttered private Catholic schools and banned priests and religious from teaching religion in public schools.

The regime's campaign against the church inspired some daring acts of resistance by clergy and laity alike. In the Diocese of Katowice in Upper Silesia, where state officials were especially zealous about eliminating religious education from the school system, Bishop Stanisław Adamski organized a petition against the effort in 1952. Citing Polish laws guaranteeing religious freedom and access to religious education, the petition demanded that religious education be restored to schools, that no obstacles be created for teachers willing to teach the subject, and that clergy not be prohibited from teaching in such schools. "This is our unshakable will," the petition read. "We will not cease demanding our rights. We will regard the failure to take our petition into account as an offense made upon us and our children, whose rearing has been entrusted to us by God, and upon future Polish generations."[17] State officials sought to stymie the petition process, but to no avail. Over 72,000 Catholics dared to pen their names on the document, knowing full well that doing so could have serious repercussions for themselves and their families. Alarmed by his impertinence and determined to make him an example, the state ordered the arrest of Adamski and two of his close associates, prevented the bishop from resuming his duties, and appointed a more pliable priest to lead the diocese in his stead. Like other attempts to beat the church into submission, however, this one only boosted its moral authority in the eyes of the general population and embarrassed the regime.

Stalin's death in 1953 touched off a power struggle in the Soviet Union, and its resolution eventually led to a softening of policy there and in many of its satellites. In Poland, Gomułka returned to power in 1956 and sought to lead the country once again down a gentler, "Polish path to socialism."[18] This initiated a distinctive phase of postwar Polish history known as the "thaw," characterized in general by an atmosphere of enhanced freedom. One of its specific features was a return of religious education, with clergy and religious as the primary instructors, as a normal feature of education.

17. Dudek, *Państwo i Kościół*, 30.
18. Diskin, *The Seeds of Triumph*.

The political climate grew colder by the early 1960s, and religious education once again served as a revealing gauge. For a regime determined to mold young Poles into lifelong supporters of the communist system, affording a prominent place to religious education in schools created too much cognitive dissonance. In 1961, in the midst of a series of transformations of the nation's educational system, the state banned religious instruction from school curricula. This policy remained in effect until the collapse of communism in 1989.

As it happens, the elimination of religious education from public schools did not mean that Polish Catholic children were not instructed in matters pertaining to the faith. It simply required clergy and lay people to create new ways for this instruction to take place, which they did with alacrity. The most notable expression of this drive was the creation of a comprehensive system of catechetical instruction based in parishes across the country.[19] By the 1970s, the content of this instruction was systematized into a program based around three four-year cycles. The program guided Catholic children through an increasingly sophisticated treatment of core Catholic teachings and challenged them to apply this teaching to moral decision-making.[20]

After 1989

Its control of public education notwithstanding, the communist party and its ideology never achieved widespread popularity in Poland, and its failure to meet the material aspirations of the population posed serious challenges to its control. By 1981 it had to resort to martial law to maintain order. Early in 1989 it agreed to generally free multiparty elections, which revealed just how bereft of appeal the PZPR had become. Poland quickly transitioned at that point from a Soviet-style, single-party state to a multiparty democracy.

The Catholic Church played a significant role in communism's collapse in Poland, and with the transition to democracy church leaders were determined to leverage the deep reservoirs of respect they enjoyed in Polish society in order to shape the country according to Catholic values. In a postcommunist context, however, the church no longer benefited from the widespread perception that it was fighting in the name of the Polish people against a disdained enemy, the communist regime. Moreover, many of its

19. Zajak and Makosa, "Poland: Faithfulness to God," 170.
20. Murawski, "Działania katechetyczne w parafii," 55–70.

priorities came to be seen as restrictions to the newly won freedoms that Poles had fought so hard to achieve. As a result, the church's political agenda generated considerable ill will, and its influence and popularity faltered.

Working with allies in government, Catholic bishops scored a series of early political victories. In August 1990, the Ministry of Education issued a decision to reintroduce religious education to elementary and high schools after a thirty-year hiatus. The policy, which is still in effect, requires all schools to provide religious education to their students. Religious organizations control the curriculum and the qualifications of instructors, and instructor salaries are funded from state coffers. Students and their parents have the right to choose to receive the instruction provided by their particular religious organization, to participate in a non-denominational ethics curriculum, or to opt out altogether. While all religious bodies have the right to provide instruction to their adherents, in practice well over ninety percent of the religion classes at every level of schooling are explicitly Catholic.[21] When the policy was introduced, critics lamented that it had emerged more or less as a surprise and without significant parliamentary debate. They also questioned its legality, although it has managed to withstand legal challenges.[22]

Responding to the disruptive potential of a free media, church leaders campaigned successfully for a provision concerning "respect for Christian values" in the radio and television broadcasting law passed in 1992. Broadcasters found guilty of violating the provision risked losing their license. The law caused considerable consternation in a society so recently liberated from a regime that had relied upon censorship of ideologically unpalatable content. Church leaders were also instrumental in the 1993 enactment of one of the toughest sets of abortion restrictions in Europe. The law, reversing relatively liberal provisions in effect since 1956, allows abortion in only three instances: when the mother's health is endangered, when the unborn child is seriously compromised, or when the pregnancy in question was the result of criminal behavior. Critics charged that the law undermined the rights of women. Later that year, church leaders celebrated the signing of a concordat between Poland and the Vatican. Framed in light of the repression experienced in the communist era, the concordat was designed to protect the religious freedom of Catholics and to promote harmonious cooperation between church and state. It contained many favorable

21. Zielińska and Zwierżdżyński, "Religious Education in Poland," 266–68.
22. Daniel, "The Church-State Situation in Poland."

provisions for the church, including state financial assistance for religious schools at the university level and for the maintenance of certain forms of church property. For critics, the obligations the concordat placed upon the state blurred the proper boundaries between church and state in a free society and privileged Catholicism over other religions.

Church leaders also actively campaigned for their preferred political candidates in the newly democratic country. This was especially clear in the 1990 presidential election, when many bishops and clergy rallied the faithful to support the successful campaign of Lech Wałęsa. Stopping just short of an official endorsement, many went to the mat for Wałęsa again in 1995 when he faced the former communist Aleksander Kwaśniewski of the Democratic Left Alliance (Sojusz Lewicy Demokratycznej), the party that emerged from the wreckage of the PZPR. Kwaśniewski's victory reflected voter discontent with Wałęsa's shortcomings as president and the painful transition to a more market-based economy over which he presided. It also indicated the limits of the church's political influence. Chastened by the result, the bishops showed more restraint in subsequent elections.

The successful reestablishment of religious education in Poland's schools thus was part of a larger pattern of political engagement by church leaders, and the substantial gains they achieved generated a similarly significant backlash. Even though the large majority of Poles identified as Catholic, many came to regard the church as overstepping its bounds in a free and democratic society. Almost from the start of the postcommunist era, sympathetic observers voiced their concerns. The widely respected philosopher Leszek Kołakowski, who while not a practicing Catholic himself, was known for his appreciation of religion's value and his respect for a theistic worldview, expressed his worries about the church's overweening ambition in an article appearing in the newspaper *Gazeta Wyborcza* in 1991.[23] Another critic was the priest and intellectual Józef Tischner, who in a 1993 article in the magazine *Tygodnik Powszechy* suggested that the church's recent course raised doubts about its commitment to democracy.[24]

One can also discern evidence of broader discontent. Polling data reveals that the church's endeavor to bring Poland's legal and political order into greater alignment with Catholic values was not very popular. In a 1991 survey, 74 percent of Poles questioned disapproved of the recent political activity of church leaders. A 1993 survey revealed that less than 40 percent

---

23. Kołakowski, "Krótka rozprawa o teokracji," 12.
24. Tischner, "Czy Kościół nas okłamał," 8–9.

supported without reservation the law reinstating religious education in schools. A poll in 1995 showed that only 32 percent supported the restrictive law on abortion.[25] Regarding attitudes toward the church in general, in a 1991 survey 58 percent identified the church as the most respected institution in Poland. That number is impressive in isolation, but less so when one considers data from 1989, when 90 percent of those questioned identified the church as the most respected institution.

It is difficult to measure how effective obligatory religious education has been in promoting Catholic identity and understanding among Polish children and young adults in the postcommunist era. It has been one element in a broad array of factors that has shaped their values and worldviews. What is clear, however, is that Polish Catholics have grown less religiously observant in recent years, and their grasp on Catholic teaching is by some measures surprisingly weak. A 1990 survey reveal that 94.2 percent of Poles were Catholics, with just 2.6 percent claiming no religion. By 2007, the same survey revealed that 88.4 percent of the population was Catholic, with 9 percent claiming no religious affiliation. A 2009 survey revealed that 41.5 percent of Polish Catholics attend Mass regularly, a rate that Catholic leaders in nearly every other country would envy. In Poland, however, this marks a substantial decline from the 1980s, when a majority of Catholics regularly fulfilled this core obligation of the faith.[26] Meanwhile, recent surveys of Polish Catholic knowledge of the essential doctrines of their religion have yielded discouraging results, leading the sociologist and priest Władysław Piwowarski to lament that two-thirds of Poles were in fact "unwitting heretics."[27]

In addition to losing influence, more recently the church in Poland has had to contend with rising levels of overt anticlericalism. One example is Palikot's Movement (Ruch Palikota, RP), a short-lived liberal political faction founded by businessman Janusz Palikot, which sought to dismantle the church's influence in Polish society. The movement's priorities included the elimination of religious education in public schools, the termination of government subsidies to Catholic organizations, the liberalization of abortion laws, and the legalization of same-sex marriage. RP proved especially popular among younger Poles, who tend to be influenced by broader European norms. In parliamentary elections in November 2011, it captured

---

25. Daniel, "The Church-State Situation in Poland," 412–15.
26. Bilska-Wodecka, "Secularization and Sacralization," 10.
27. Lewandowski, "Oto Polak," 36–39.

around 10 percent of the vote, an impressive figure for so young a movement in its first political contest.

Conclusion

Polish society participated in the educational revolution that has transformed much of the modern world: the requirement that all children and young adults pass through many years of general education designed to forge them into loyal citizens capable of flourishing in a dynamic industrial economy that emphasizes the management of knowledge, frequent adaptation, and serial specialization. The state claimed a growing role in managing the complex systems that provided universal education, in part because it had the capacity to do so, and in part because the stakes involved made such management politically expedient.

The Catholic Church in Poland and elsewhere was hardly indifferent to the growing educational brief of the state, and it defended its traditional prerogatives. This defense was rooted in the Catholic understanding of education's function in the cultivation not just of patriotism and productivity but also piety, a vibrant religious belief and discipline conducive to salvation. In Poland, the church's track record in preserving its claims was decidedly mixed. While the substantial majority of Poles were Catholic, throughout much of the nineteenth and twentieth centuries the Polish people were ruled by regimes hostile to the church and its educational vision.

The irony of this history is that the church was often more successful in forming faithful Catholics when it faced concerted opposition from the state. In the Prussian/German partition, and again in the communist era, when the government reduced or eliminated the church's role in education, Catholics tended to rally to the church's defense, giving rise to creative educational initiatives that fostered vibrant connections with the faith. When the church managed to reassert its vision, such as in the interwar period and more recently in the postcommunist period, it generated resentment among Catholics and non-Catholics alike, rooted in the conviction that the church was exceeding its proper limits within the context of a free and democratic society.

On a universal level, the Catholic Church gradually has made something akin to peace with the modern transformation of education, including its predominantly secular focus and the high degree of state control. A landmark in the evolution of its thinking is the declaration *Gravissimum*

Educationis, issued at the tail end of the Second Vatican Council in 1965. The document revisits the terrain staked out by Pius XI's 1929 encyclical, but with some noteworthy shifts in emphasis. It begins with the recognition that education has come to belong to the "secular part" of the human experience. "Holy Mother the Church must be concerned with the whole of man's life, even the secular part of it insofar as it has a bearing on his heavenly calling. Therefore she has a role in the progress and development of education." The council fathers grant that every person has "an inalienable right to an education," and a proper education includes religion. Young people have a right "to appraise moral values with a right conscience, to embrace them with a personal adherence, together with a deeper knowledge and love of God." For their part, Christian youth have "a right to a Christian education." The declaration acknowledges the claims of the family and the church in education, but these are not as paramount as Pius XI would have it. The council fathers admit that "certain rights and duties belong indeed to civil society, whose role is to direct what is required for the common temporal good." Rather than calling upon the state to defer to family and church, the declaration holds out the hope for harmonious co-operation. "Therefore the state must protect the right of children to an adequate school education, check on the ability of teachers and the excellence of their training, look after the health of the pupils and in general, promote the whole school project. But it must always keep in mind the principle of subsidiarity so that there is no kind of school monopoly, for this is opposed to the native rights of the human person, to the development and spread of culture, to the peaceful association of citizens and to the pluralism that exists today in ever so many societies."[28]

Gravissimum Educationis emerged in the context of Vatican II, a remarkable experience in which global Catholic leaders displayed a heightened openness to contemporary culture and sought to bring Catholic teaching and praxis into creative conversation with that culture. During the council and its aftermath, the church in Poland remained locked in a high-stakes contest with a hostile state, and this struggle insulated it to a considerable degree from the new ethos at work in the global church. The defensiveness and militancy that served the church in Poland well during communism has continued to manifest in the postcommunist era, and there is mounting evidence to suggest that it has led to considerable discord. By many measures, the Catholic Church in Poland continues to thrive, but

---

28. Second Vatican Council, *Gravissimum Educationis*.

as it advances its mission it would do well to learn from its history and to remain attuned to the signs of the times. Insisting on religious education in public schools and the church's control over its content and instructors may carry costs that outweigh the benefit of these policies.

Bibliography

Adamski, Stanisław, ed. *Szkoła wedle nauki Kościoła i uchwał synodu*. Katowice: Śląsk, 1939.
Alvis, Robert E. *Religion and the Rise of Nationalism: A Profile of an East-Central European City*. Syracuse, NY: Syracuse University Press, 2005.
Bilska-Wodecka, Elżbieta. "Secularization and Sacralization: New Polarization of the Polish Religious Landscape in the Context of Globalization and European Integration." *Geographica* 44 (2009) 3–18.
Daniel, Krystyna. "The Church-State Situation in Poland After the Collapse of Communism." *Brigham Young University Law Review* 1995 (1995) 401–19.
Diskin, Hanna. *The Seeds of Triumph: Church and State in Gomułka's Poland*. Budapest: Central European University Press, 2001.
Dudek, Antoni. *Państwo i kościół w Polsce 1945–1970*. Cracow: PiT, 1995.
Gellner, Ernest. *Nations and Nationalism*. Ithaca, NY: Cornell University Press, 1983.
Hagan, William W. *Germans, Poles, and Jews: The Nationality Conflict in the Prussian East, 1772–1914*. Chicago: University of Chicago Press, 1980.
Janowski, Andrzej. "Polish Education: Changes and Prospects." In *Education and Economic Change in Eastern Europe and the Former Soviet Union*, edited by David Phillips and Michael Kaser, 41–55. Wallingford, UK: Triangle, 1993.
Kołakowski, Leszek. "Krótka rozprawa o teokracji." *Gazeta Wyborcza* 197 (August 24, 1991) 12.
Korth, Rudolf. *Die preussische Schulpolitik und die polnischen Schulstreiks: Ein Beitrag zur preussischen Polenpolitik der Ära Bülow*. Würzburg: Holzner, 1963.
Lewandowski, Edmund. "Oto Polak." *Polityka* 16 (April 19, 2007) 36–39.
Michnik, Adam. *The Church and the Left*. Edited, translated, and with an introduction by David Ost. Chicago: University of Chicago Press, 1993.
Murawski, Roman. "Działania katechetyczne w parafii w świetle Dyrektorium Ogólnego i Polskiego." In *Przesłanie dokumentów katechetycznych Kościoła w Polsce*, edited by Stanisław Dziekoński, 55–70. Warsaw: Verbinum, 2003.
Second Vatican Council. *Gravissimum Educationis*. http://www.vatican.va/archive/hist_councils/ii_vatican_council/documents/vat-ii_decl_19651028_gravissimum-educationis_en.html.
Szczepaniak, Jan. *Episkopat w obronie katolickiego charakteru polskiej szkoły w latach 1927–1937*. Cracow: "Unum," 2000.
———. *Troska Kościoła o nauczanie i wychowanie religijne w szkole w latach 1918–1927*. Cracow: WAM, 1997.
Tischner, Józef. "Czy Kościół nas okłamał...?" *Tygodnik Powszechny* 2 (January 10, 1993) 8–9.
Truchim, Stefan. *Historia szkolnictwa i oświaty w Wielkim Księstwie Poznańskim, 1815–1915*. 2 vols. Łódź: Zakład Narodowy im. Ossolińskich, 1967.

Ulich, Robert. *A History of Religious Education: Documents and Interpretations from the Judaeo-Christian Tradition*. New York: New York University Press, 1968.

Zajac, Marian, and Paweł Makosa. "Poland: Faithfulness to God and to People." In *How Teachers in Europe Teach Religion: An International Empirical Study in 16 Countries*, edited by Hans-Georg Ziebertz and Ulrich Riegel, 169–80. Berlin: Lit, 2009.

Zielińska, Katarzyna and Marcin K. Zwierżdżyński. "Religious Education in Poland." In *The Routledge International Handbook of Religious Education*, edited by Derek H. Davis and Elena Miroshnikova, 264–71. New York: Routledge, 2013.

4

Christian Education

Rights and Obligations in Light of the
1983 Code of Canon Law[1]

—Fr. Patrick Cooney, OSB

Introduction

MEMBERSHIP IN THE CATHOLIC Church comes with the basic obligations of cooperating in the building up of the Body of Christ,[2] of maintaining communion with the church,[3] and directing one's efforts to lead a holy life and promote the growth of the church.[4] But how is one to maintain this communion and grow in the faith unless one seeks knowledge, skills, and understanding, which for the Christian faithful comes through a

---

1. All references to the Code of Canon Law will be taken from Catholic Church, *Code of Canon Law*, Latin-English Edition (Washington, DC: Canon Law Society of America, 1999).

2. Canon (c.) 208: "From their rebirth in Christ, there exists among all the Christian faithful a true equality regarding dignity and action by which they all cooperate in the building up of the Body of Christ according to each one's own condition and function."

3. C. 209: "§1. The Christian faithful, even in their own manner of acting, are always obliged to maintain communion with the Church. §2. With great diligence they are to fulfill the duties which they owe to the universal Church and the particular church to which they belong according to the prescripts of the law."

4. C. 210: "All the Christian faithful must direct their efforts to lead a holy life and to promote the growth of the Church and its continual sanctification, according to their own condition."

Christian education? Like the fig tree in St. Luke's Gospel (13:1–9), we are called to cultivate the ground around it and fertilize it so that it may bear fruit in the future. Without a Christian education, the faithful will be unable to bear fruit in building up the church and enlivening the ministry of evangelization.

The importance and necessity of Christian education are inextricably tied to one's membership in the community of faith, and it is this membership, established through the sacrament of baptism, that carries certain rights and obligations. One such right and obligation is the exercising and fulfilling of a Christian and Catholic education. Parents, bishops, priests, and the laity are obliged to assist in the achievement of this right, either personally or by providing the resources to assist others in meeting this obligation. This chapter addresses the right to a Christian education and who is obligated to ensure this right is achieved, namely, parents, pastors of souls (bishops and priests), those who assist these pastors, and finally the faith community itself.

The Basic Right and Obligation for All to an Education

In the introduction to the Second Vatican Council's *Gravissimum Educationis*, the Council Fathers speak of how the "rights of men to an education, particularly the primary rights of children and parents, are being proclaimed and recognized in public documents."[5] The footnote to their statement points particularly to the inalienable right to an education, which was adopted by the General Assembly of the United Nations in their 1948 Declaration on the Rights of Man.[6] *Gravissimum Educationis* states, "All . . . in virtue of their dignity as human persons, have an inalienable right to education."[7] It states further that "all Christians—that is, all those who having been reborn in water and the Holy Spirit are called and in fact are children of God—have a right to a Christian education."[8] So Catholics not only have a right to an education, they also have a right to a Christian education, which the church has codified in canon 217 of the 1983 Code of Canon Law: "Since they are called by baptism to lead a life in keeping

---

5. Vatican II, *Gravissimum Educationis*, Introduction.

6. See Article 26 of *The Universal Declaration of Human Rights*, adopted by the United Nations General Assembly on 10 December 1948.

7. Vatican II, *Gravissimum Educationis*, 1.

8. Ibid.

with the teaching of the gospel, the Christian faithful have the right to a Christian education by which they are to be instructed properly to strive for the maturity of the human person and at the same time to know and live the mystery of salvation."[9]

This right to a Christian education is based on one's dignity as a human person and on the duty of the baptized to live an evangelical life.[10] But what exactly is Christian education that would enable persons to live a life of discipleship? In his encyclical *Divini Illus Magistri*, Pope Pius XI states: "it is clear that there can be no true education which is not wholly directed to man's last end, and that in the present order of Providence, since God has revealed Himself to us in the Person of His Only Begotten Son, who alone is 'the way, the truth and the life,' there can be no ideally perfect education which is not Christian education."[11] This is echoed in *Gravissimum Educationis*: "True education is directed towards the formation of the human person in view of his final end and the good of that society to which he belongs and in the duties of which he will, as an adult, have a share."[12] The document then speaks to what this education entails: a harmonious development of physical, moral, and intellectual endowments; sexual education; training in the skills that lead to community involvement; an ability for discourse; an ability to promote the common good; and an ability to appraise moral values with a right conscience, to embrace and adhere to them from a deeper knowledge of God. The aim of such an education is not just limited to the teaching of theory, but also to the maturity of the human person and as well as the knowledge of and lived experience of the mystery of salvation.

Christian education is an invitation to Christians to participate "in their own way in Christ's priestly, prophetic, and royal function" and "to exercise the mission which God has entrusted to the church to fulfill in the world, in accord with the condition proper to each."[13] This education begins with children, so that they grow up as members of the church. In his apostolic exhortation *Familiaris consortio* (The Christian Family in the Modern World), Pope John Paul II states:

---

9. Cenalmor, "Obligations and Rights," 109–13.
10. Provost, "Obligations and Rights," 155.
11. Pius XI, *Divini Illus Magistri*, 7.
12. Vatican II, *Gravissimum Educationis*, 1.
13. C. 204, §1.

> *Remote preparation* begins in early childhood, in that wise family training which leads children to discover themselves as beings endowed with a rich and complex psychology and with a particular personality with its own strengths and weaknesses. It is the period when esteem for all authentic human values is instilled, both in interpersonal and in social relationships, with all that this signifies for the formation of character, for the control and right use of one's inclinations, for the manner of regarding and meeting people of the opposite sex, and so on. Also necessary, especially for Christians, is solid spiritual and catechetical formation that will show that marriage is a true vocation and mission, without excluding the possibility of the total gift of self to God in the vocation to the priestly or religious life.[14]

Pope John Paul II points to the importance of early childhood formation, a formation that even at this stage is molding the child in a Catholic Christian environment, an education to which every Christian child has a right.

The Code of Canon Law also speaks of the obligation to obtain a Christian education, an obligation that doesn't stop when one has come of age. According to canon 225, for instance, the lay Christian faithful are called to bring the gospel message of Jesus Christ into the workplace. This canon states:

> §1. Since, like all the Christian faithful, lay persons are designated by God for the apostolate through baptism and confirmation, they are bound by the general obligation and possess the right as individuals, or joined in associations, to work so that the divine message of salvation is made known and accepted by all persons everywhere in the world. This obligation is even more compelling in those circumstances in which only through them can people hear the gospel and know Christ.
>
> §2. According to each one's own condition, they are also bound by a particular duty to imbue and perfect the order of temporal affairs with the spirit of the gospel and thus to give witness to Christ, especially in carrying out these same affairs and in exercising secular functions.

The laity cannot successfully carry out their obligations unless they have been prepared and educated in their faith.

---

14. John Paul II, *Familiaris consortio*, 66.

Those Responsible to See to the Fulfillment of the Right to a Christian Education

As Pope John Paul II alluded to in *Familiaris consortio*, education begins in the family. The Code of Canon Law makes it quite clear that the family has not only the right but also the most serious (*gravissima*) responsibility of educating their children (c. 226, §2). But parents are not alone in this responsibility. The Code of Canon Law points to others who are obligated to support parents in this regard and in some cases to step in if the parents are unable or fail to live up to their responsibility. This obligation includes those who are charged with the care of souls (diocesan bishops, pastors, and chaplains), catechists, and the entire faith community. As Pope Pius XI put it in his encyclical *Divini Illius Magistri*, "Education is essentially a social and not a mere individual activity."[15]

The Obligations of Parents

The group primarily responsible for educating children is parents. It is through the education of their children that "parents realize in a concrete fashion the mandate given to all the faithful in canon 835, §4, to participate in the sanctifying work of the people of God."[16] This and other canons take their cue from conciliar documents. For instance, the Second Vatican Council's *Lumen Gentium* (Dogmatic Constitution on the Church) states:

> From the marriage of Christians there comes the family in which new citizens of human society are born and, by the grace of the Holy Spirit in Baptism, those are made children of God so that the People of God may be perpetuated throughout the centuries. In what might be regarded as the domestic Church, the parents, by word and example, are the first heralds of the faith with regard to their children. They must foster the vocation which is proper to each child, and this with special care if it be to religion.[17]

Gravissimum Educationis articulates it this way:

> As it is the parents who have given life to their children, on them lies the gravest obligation of educating their family. They must

---

15. Pius XI, *Divini Illus Magistri*, 11.
16. Baillargeon, "Rights and Duties of Parents," 55–56.
17. Vatican II, *Lumen Gentium*, 11.

therefore be recognized as being primarily and principally responsible for their education. The role of parents in education is of such importance that it is almost impossible to provide an adequate substitute.[18]

The Code of Canon Law is faithful to these documents by not only acknowledging the importance of parents in the education of their children but also enshrining this in church law. Canon 226, §2 states: "Since they have given life to their children, parents have a most grave obligation and possess the right to educate them. Therefore, it is for Christian parents particularly to take care of the Christian education of their children according to the doctrine handed on by the Church." By virtue of giving life to children, parents are obliged to ensure their education.

How is this right and obligation to be lived out by parents? *Gravissimum Educationis* explains:

> The family is therefore the principal school of the social virtues which are necessary to every society. It is therefore above all in the Christian family, inspired by the grace and the responsibility of the sacrament of matrimony, that children should be taught to know and worship God and to love their neighbor, in accordance with the faith which they have received in earliest infancy in the sacrament of Baptism. In it, also, they will have their first experience of a well-balanced human society and of the Church. Finally it is through the family that they are gradually initiated into association with their fellow-men in civil life and as members of the people of God. Parents should, therefore, appreciate how important a role the truly Christian family plays in the life and progress of the whole people of God.[19]

These areas of formation also find further expression in the Code of Canon Law. Canon 1136, which speaks of the "Effects of Marriage," states that parents have a most grave duty (*officium gravissimum*) in and primary right (*ius primarium*) of the education of their children. Parents fulfill this right and duty by taking "care as best they can for the physical, social, cultural, moral, and religious education of their offspring." Canon 774, §2 addresses the education of the whole person, which begins with the parents' obligation to "form their children by word and example in faith and in the practice of Christian life." Once the children reach school age, canon 793, §1 states

---

18. Vatican II, *Gravissimum Educationis*, 3.
19. Ibid.

that parents have the right and obligation of "choosing those means and institutions through which they can provide more suitably for the Catholic education of their children."

By fulfilling their right and obligation regarding education, parents participate in a special way in the sanctifying office of the church, which is seen most clearly in the sacraments. Broadly stated, "It is in fact for parents to begin the religious initiation of the child, to teach it to love Christ as a close friend and to form its conscience."[20] This religious initiation and sanctifying function are seen in the sacrament of baptism by the requirement of the parents "to be instructed properly on the meaning of this sacrament and the obligations attached to it" (c. 851, 2°).

The parental role is further realized in the sacrament of confirmation. Canon 890 reminds parents that they are to take care that their children are both "properly instructed to receive the sacrament and come to it at the appropriate time." This canon helps to put into action what is spelled out about their role in the Rite of Confirmation:

> The initiation of children into the sacramental life is ordinarily the responsibility and concern of Christian parents. They are to form and gradually increase a spirit of faith in the children and, at times with the help of catechism classes, prepare them for the fruitful reception of the sacraments of confirmation and eucharist. The role of the parents is also expressed by their active participation in the celebration of the sacraments.[21]

Yet another sacramental feature of the parents' obligations in the formation of their children is the Eucharist. Canon 914 states that it is "primarily the duty of parents" to see that their children who have reached the use of reason are prepared properly, have made sacramental confession, and then receive their first communion as soon as possible. The *National Directory for Catechesis* highlights the importance of the role of the parents and family: "Children's preparation for first reception of Eucharist begins in the home. The family has the most important role in communicating the Christian and human values that form the foundation for a child's understanding of the Eucharist. Children who participate with their family in the Mass experience the Eucharistic mystery in an initial way and gradually learn to join with the liturgical assembly in prayer."[22]

20. SCDF, *Pastoralis Actio*, 32.
21. Catholic Church, "Rite of Confirmation," 3.
22. USCCB, *National Directory for Catechesis*, 3a.

The Obligations of the Church and "Pastors of Souls"

Besides parents, there are others in the church who have a role and duty to provide a Catholic and Christian education to those in the church. This call to educate begins first with the church as an institution. Council Fathers at the Second Vatican Council stressed the obligation of the church, as mother, to provide its children with an education along with the assistance needed to promote the well-balanced perfection of persons, for the good of society and the developing of a world more worthy of God's creation. This special concern of the church was codified in canon 794. The first paragraph of this canon states, "The duty and right of educating belongs in a special way to the church, to which has been divinely entrusted the mission of assisting persons so that they are able to reach the fullness of the Christian life." This finds its expression in *Gravissimum Educationis:*

> Education is, in a very special way, the concern of the Church, not only because the Church must be recognized as a human society capable of imparting education, but especially it has the duty of proclaiming the way of salvation to all men, of revealing the life of Christ to those who believe, and of assisting them with unremitting care so that they may be able to attain to the fullness of that life.[23]

While the church is concerned with Christian education, canon 794 specifically points to the duty of those who are "pastors of souls" in arranging a Catholic education for the faithful under their care. One way in which this education is accomplished is through catechesis. Canon 773 states, "It is a proper and grave duty especially of pastors of souls" to see to the catechetical needs of the faithful, so that their faith can become "manifest and active through doctrinal instruction and the experience of Christian life."[24] *Gravissimum Educationis* elaborates further that catechesis is important because it "illumines and strengthens the faith, develops a life in harmony with the spirit of Christ, stimulates a conscious and fervent participation in the liturgical mystery and encourages men to take an active part in the apostolate."[25]

At the diocesan level, it is the bishop who is to be concerned about catechesis. *Christus Dominus* states that:

---

23. Vatican II, *Gravissimum Educationis*, 3.
24. C. 773.
25. Vatican II, *Gravissimum Educationis*, 4.

> Bishops should be especially concerned about catechetical instruction. Its function is to develop in men a living, explicit and active faith, enlightened by doctrine. It should be very carefully imparted, not only to children and adolescents but also to young people and even to adults. In imparting this instruction the teachers must observe an order and method suited not only to the matter in hand but also to the character, the ability, the age and the life-style of their audience. This instruction should be based on holy scripture, tradition, liturgy, and on the teaching authority and life of the Church.[26]

This concern is addressed as well in canon 775, which states that bishops are to issue norms for catechesis and are to make available suitable means of providing and coordinating catechesis in their dioceses.[27] The law even allows, if it is opportune, for the bishop to prepare his own catechism.[28] For instance, Pope John Paul II reiterates this point in his apostolic exhortation *Catechesi tradendae* (Catechesis in our Time), stating: "Your principal role will be to bring about and maintain in your Churches a real passion for catechesis, a passion embodied in a pertinent and effective organization, putting into operation the necessary personnel, means and equipment, and also financial resources."[29]

Yet another way that bishops show this concern is their charge of caring for their catechists. Canon 780 states that this care is to begin with their preparation and extend through continuing education so that catechists "understand the doctrine of the Church appropriately, and that they learn in theory and in practice the methods proper to the teaching disciplines."[30]

In addition to addressing the bishop's role in catechesis, John Paul II addresses the catechetical role of priests, who in catechesis are immediate assistants to their bishops:

> For your part, priests, here you have a field in which you are the immediate assistants of your Bishops. The Council has called you "instructors in the faith"; there is no better way for you to be such instructors than by devoting your best efforts to the growth of your communities in the faith. Whether you are in charge of a parish, or are chaplains to primary or secondary schools or universities, or

---

26. Vatican II, *Christus Dominus*, 14.
27. C. 775, §1.
28. Ibid.
29. John Paul II, *Catechesi tradendae*, 63.
30. C. 780.

have responsibility for pastoral activity at any level, or are leaders of large or small communities, especially youth groups, the Church expects you to neglect nothing with a view to a well-organized and well-oriented catechetical effort.[31]

The priest, as pastor, is obligated at the parish level with the catechetical formation of adults, youth, and children.[32] Canon 528 states that the pastor is "obligated to make provision so that the word of God is proclaimed in its entirety to those living in the parish; for this reason, he is to take care that the lay members of the Christian faithful are instructed in the truths of the faith, especially by giving a homily on Sundays and holy days of obligation and by offering catechetical instruction." This obligation, as was seen above in canon 773, is the grave duty of making sure that the job gets done; it is one of the most serious obligations of a pastor.[33]

The pastor needs to understand that the goal of catechesis is to make manifest and active the living faith of Christians so that it can be a guiding force in their lives. The process of catechesis "accomplishes this end by means of 'the experience of Christian life' as well as by doctrinal formation."[34] It is by interacting with others, be it Christian families, one's neighborhood, school or local church, that a person gains the experience and learning that comes with living out one's faith. Liturgical catechesis is an integral part of this ongoing formation in Christ. Canon 777, 1° speaks to the continuous catechesis that is required to support the sacramental life of the parish. Coriden notes how "the canon illustrates the close interrelation between the teaching and sanctifying offices in the Church; sacramental catechesis is one point at which the two coincide."[35] This sacramental catechesis and explanations of the sacraments are given both for and on the occasion of sacramental celebrations.[36] Canon 843, §2 reiterates this when it states, "Pastors of souls ... have the duty to take care that those who seek the sacraments are prepared to receive them by proper evangelization and catechetical instruction." These instructions and explanations "may be long or short, e.g., a six-week series in preparation for confirmation or a few words before Mass

---

31. John Paul II, *Catechesi tradendae*, 64.

32. C. 776.

33. Coriden, "Catechetical Instruction," 933–34. Also see canons 386, §1, 538, §1, and 843, §2 that reiterate this duty.

34. Ibid., 934.

35. Ibid., 936.

36. Coriden, *The Code of Canon Law*, 558–59.

or the anointing of the sick. It is an ongoing and challenging form of pastoral catechesis, and one of the most important. The faithful must understand what they celebrate in the sacraments so that they may participate actively and intelligently."[37] Canon 777 expands this idea of catechesis from that of the first sacraments to stressing the importance of catechizing all, including the mentally and physically handicapped, and finally 5°, stressing that the catechesis of adults, which according to the *General Catechetical Directory* (1971), "must be accepted as the principal kind of catechesis, towards which all other forms, while always needed, are directed."[38]

It is important to highlight 4°, which speaks to the catechesis of "those who are physically or mentally impeded." There are no specifics about how this is to be done in the canons, but mention is made in the *General Catechetical Directory*, which states:

> This task may not be relegated to a secondary or subsidiary place. Handicapped children and adolescents constitute no small proportion of our citizens. Present-day conditions in society make it difficult, very often, for young people to develop properly and to adjust properly to society. Catechesis must offer these the possibility of living the life of faith in keeping with their state. This is an eminently evangelical task and a most important witness, a constant in the tradition of the Church.[39]

The Code of Canon Law directly addresses sacramental instruction for the sacraments of baptism, confirmation, Eucharist, and marriage. The sacraments, in short, become opportunities for Christian education. The baptism of children, according to canon 867, speaks of the requirement of the proper preparation of the parents, though this preparation is not spelled out. Baptism of adults is addressed by canon 855, §1 which states that the sacramental instruction of adults is to address the truths of faith and the obligations taken on through baptism.[40] This sacramental preparation takes place through the process of the Rite of Christian Initiation of Adults in the parish. Preparation for confirmation is addressed by canon 889, §2, which states that suitable instruction is required for the licit reception of the sacrament. Canon 890, which is addressed to pastors, states, "pastors of parishes, are to take care that the faithful are properly instructed

---

37. Ibid.
38. SCC, *Ad normam decreti*, 20.
39. Ibid.
40. C. 855, §1.

to receive the sacrament and come to it at the appropriate time." The sacrament of the Most Holy Eucharist, called the most august sacrament,[41] and which is to be held in the highest honor, requires, as stated in canon 898, that pastors of souls instruct the faithful about the doctrine of the sacraments, the diligent obligation of taking an active part in the sacrament, and its devout and frequent reception.

Another occasion for Christian education is the sacrament of marriage. Canon 1063 addresses marriage, stating that "Pastors of souls are obliged to take care that their ecclesiastical community offers the Christian faithful the assistance by which the matrimonial state is preserved in a Christian spirit and advances in perfection." Instruction on the sacrament of marriage entails much more than catechesis before the union; it must also influence the fruitful celebration of the sacrament and continue into the very marriage itself.

Though there is no direct requirement in the Code of Canon Law for sacramental instruction for the sacraments of penance and anointing, the pastor is still charged with the serious responsibility of ensuring that the members of the parish receive instruction. For instance, canon 987 on the sacrament of penance states that, "To receive the salvific remedy of the sacrament of penance, a member of the Christian faithful must be disposed in such a way that, rejecting sins committed and having a purpose of amendment, the person is turned back to God." The penitent, in order to meet the obligations of the sacrament, has to have been instructed on the meaning and proper manner for receiving the sacrament.[42] The sacrament of anointing of the sick also has no direct requirements for sacramental instruction; however, canon 1002 does call for instruction for the communal celebration of the sacrament. It states, "The communal celebration of the anointing of the sick for many of the sick at once, who have been suitably prepared and are properly disposed, can be performed according to the prescripts of the diocesan bishop."

In short, bishops and priests, especially diocesan bishops and pastors, in their duty of caring for souls, are charged with the serious duty of ensuring that those in their care receive a Christian education. As illustrated above, this is done either directly through catechesis or indirectly through their support of the parents. In meeting their duty, they very often seek the assistance of others.

41. C. 897.
42. CC. 987–88.

In meeting their obligation of educating the Christian faithful, pastors are not expected to do it alone. Canon 776 encourages them to "use the help of the clerics attached to the parish, of members of institutes of consecrated life and of societies of apostolic life . . . and of lay members of the Christian faithful, especially of catechists. None of these are to refuse to offer their help willingly unless they are legitimately impeded." Though this canon calls for the pastor to enlist the assistance of others, it still places the central and coordinating responsibility on the pastor, as well as highlighting that the catechetical concerns of adults, youth and children are to be his main concern.[43]

Canon 776 identifies three groups that are called to aid the pastor. The first group is clerics attached to the parish, which would include associate pastors and those who may be in residence. The second group is religious, when the nature of their life allows their involvement in catechesis.[44] "The dedication of religious men and women to the task of religious instruction," the canon states, "is appropriate because of their consecration of God and their life of witnessing to Christ."[45] The final group is lay members of the Christian faithful, especially catechists. Canon 785, §1 avers, "catechists are lay members of the Christian faithful, duly instructed and outstanding in Christian life, who devote themselves to setting forth the teaching of the gospel and to organizing liturgies and works of charity." John Paul II asserts in *Catechesi tradendae*: "We must be grateful to the Lord for this contribution by the laity, but it is also a challenge to our responsibility as pastors, since these lay catechists must be carefully prepared for what is, if not a formally instituted ministry, at the very least a function of great importance in the Church."[46]

Catechists, whose role is to provide direct catechetical instruction to the faithful, can fulfill this function in one of two ways. A catechist can either fulfill this role personally, fulfilling their duty as outlined in canon 225, §1,[47] or officially as a public catechist of the church receiving an official

---

43. Coriden, *The Code of Canon Law*, 557–58.

44. For example, a contemplative community's nature, i.e. cloistered nuns or monks, would mitigate against catechetical involvement.

45. Coriden, *The Code of Canon Law*, 557–58.

46. John Paul II, *Catechesi tradendae*, 71.

47. C. 225: "§1. Since, like all the Christian faithful, lay persons are designated by God for the apostolate through baptism and confirmation, they are bound by the general obligation and possess the right as individuals, or joined in associations, to work so that the divine message of salvation is made known and accepted by all persons everywhere

catechetical mission. When a person functions in a non-official role as a catechist, other than the general canon laws that pertain to catechists, there are no specific legal requirements. The second type of catechists, those who have an official or public role as a catechist in the church, may require greater supervision because of the nature of their role.[48]

Besides catechists, there are also those designated and employed as teachers, who teach in Catholic schools and who "must remember that it depends chiefly on them whether the Catholic school achieves its purpose."[49] According to canon 796, §2, teachers and parents are to cooperate together in the education of children, "teachers in fulfilling their duty are to collaborate very closely with parents, who are to be heard willingly and for whom associations or meetings are to be established and highly esteemed." As to their qualifications, canon 802, §2 states that "teachers are to be outstanding in correct doctrine and integrity of life." This is because the instruction and education that occurs in Catholic schools is to be grounded in the principles of Catholic doctrine. This is spelled out in more detail in *Gravissimum Educationis*:

> Possessed by charity both towards each other and towards their pupils, and inspired by an apostolic spirit, they should bear testimony by their lives and their teaching to the one Teacher, who is Christ. Above all they should work in close cooperation with the parents. In the entire educational program they should, together with the parents, make full allowance for the difference of sex and for the particular role which providence has appointed to each sex in the family and in society. They should strive to awaken in their pupils a spirit of personal initiative and, even after they have left school, they should continue to help them with their advice and friendship and by the organization of special groups imbued with the true spirit of the Church. The sacred Synod declares that the services of such teachers constitute an active apostolate, one which is admirably suited to our times and indeed is very necessary.[50]

Teachers are necessary in the shared cooperation of providing religious education to children.

---

in the world. This obligation is even more compelling in those circumstances in which only through them can people hear the gospel and know Christ."

48. Fuentes, "Catechetical Formation," 133–36.

49. Vatican II, *Gravissimum Educationis*, 8.

50. Ibid.

Though the Code of Canon Law singles out certain groups, such as parents, pastors, and catechists, it also calls upon all of the Christian faithful to assist in Christian education. Canon 774, §1 states, "Under the direction of legitimate ecclesiastical authority, solicitude for catechesis belongs to all members of the Church according to each one's role." The health and vigor of the church relies on the concern of every believer to the catechetical effort. Canon 774 is based on the participation of all believers in the prophetic office of Christ.[51] This participation is described in *Lumen Gentium*:

> The holy People of God shares also in Christ's prophetic office: it spreads abroad a living witness to him, especially by a life of faith and love and by offering to God a sacrifice of praise, the fruit of lips praising his name.... This characteristic is shown in the supernatural appreciation of the faith (*sensus fidei*) of the whole people, when, "from the bishops to the last of the faithful" they manifest a universal consent in matters of faith and morals.[52]

It is through this prophetic role as stated in canon 211 that "all the Christian faithful have the duty and right to work so that the divine message of salvation more and more reaches all people in every age and in every land." Canon 225, §1 asserts that "lay persons are designated by God for the apostolate... they are bound by the general obligation and possess the right as individuals, or joined in associations, to work so that the divine message of salvation is made known and accepted by all persons everywhere in the world." The Vatican II decree *Apostolicam Actuositatem* (On the Apostolate of Lay People), also states:

> Participators in the function of Christ, priest, prophet and king, the laity have an active part of their own in the life and action of the Church. Their action within the Church communities is so necessary that without it the apostolate of the pastors will frequently be unable to obtain its full effect.... They engage zealously in its apostolic works; they draw men towards the Church who had been perhaps very far away from it; they ardently cooperate in the spread of the Word of God, particularly by catechetical instruction; by their expert assistance they increase the efficacy of the care of souls as well as of the administration of the goods of the Church.[53]

---

51. Coriden, *The Code of Canon Law*, 555–56.
52. Vatican II, *Lumen Gentium*, 12.
53. Vatican II, *Apostolicam Actuositatem*, 10.

The role of the faith community, then, is crucial to ensure that the right to a Christian education is not only recognized but is assured. Thus every member of the church has not just a right to a Christian education but has a role to play in Christian education.

Conclusion

The right to an education is an inalienable right that comes by birth. More particularly, the right to a Christian education arises from baptism, and thus allows one to meet the obligations that accompany this sacrament. These obligations include cooperating in the building up of the Body of Christ, maintaining communion with the church, and directing one's efforts to lead a holy life and promote the growth of the church. The right to a Christian education is not new, but it has taken on a fresh and renewed emphasis through the documents of the Second Vatican Council and the 1983 Code of Canon Law, which focused at length on the topic. These documents emphasize that the church as a whole, both as an institution and those who make up that institution, is responsible for making Christian education available so that individuals and communities can live a life of discipleship, witnessing the love and compassion of Christ to the world.

Bibliography

Anderson, Bernhard W., et al. *The New Oxford Annotated Bible with the Apocryphal/Deuterocanonical Books*. New York: Oxford University Press, 1994.

Baillargeon, Paul E. "The Rights and Duties of Parents in the Sanctification of Their Children." *CLSA Proceedings* 54 (1992) 55–71.

Beal, John P. et al., eds. *New Commentary on the Code of Canon Law*. Mahwah, NJ: Paulist, 2000.

Caparros, Ernest. "Title II: The Obligations and Rights of the Lay Members of Christ's Faithful (cc. 224–231)." In *Code of Canon Law Annotated*, edited by Ernest Caparros et al., 152–201. Montreal: Wilson & Lafleur, 1993.

Caparros, Ernest, et al. *Exegetical Commentary on the Code of Canon Law*. Montreal: Wilson & Lafleur, 2004.

Caparros, Ernest, et al., eds. *Code of Canon Law Annotated*. Montreal: Wilson & Lafleur, 1993.

Catholic Church. *Code of Canon Law*. Latin-English Edition. Washington, DC: Canon Law Society of America, 1999.

Catholic Church. "Rite of Confirmation." In *The Rites of the Catholic Church*, vol. 1, 469–515. Collegeville, MN: Liturgical, 2001.

Catholic Church. *The Rites of the Catholic Church*. Collegeville, MN: Liturgical, 1990.

Cenalmor, Daniel. "Title I: The Obligations and Rights of all Christ's Faithful." In *Code of Canon Law Annotated*, edited by Ernest Caparros et al., 35–151. Montreal: Wilson & Lafleur, 1993.

Coriden, James, A. "Catechetical Instruction (cc. 773–780)." In *The Code of Canon Law: A Text and Commentary*, edited by James A. Coriden et al., 555–59. Mahwah, NJ: Paulist, 1985.

———. "Catechetical Instruction [cc. 773–780]." In *New Commentary on the Code of Canon Law*, ed. John P. Beal, et al., 933–37. Mahwah, NJ: Paulist, 2000.

Coriden, James, et al., eds. *The Code of Canon Law: A Text and Commentary*. Mahwah, NJ: Paulist, 1985.

Flannery, Austin, ed. *Vatican Council II*, vol. 1, *The Conciliar and Post Conciliar Documents*. Northport, NY: Costello, 1998.

———, ed. *Vatican Council II*, vol. 2, *More Post Conciliar Documents*. Northport, NY: Costello, 1998.

Fuentes, José A. "Catechetical Formation (cc. 773–780)." In *Code of Canon Law Annotated*, edited by Ernest Caparros et al., 107–36. Montreal: Wilson & Lafleur, 1993.

John Paul II. *Catechesi tradendae*. In *Vatican Council II*, vol. 2, *More Post Conciliar Documents*, edited by Austin Flannery, 762–814. Northport, NY: Costello, 1998.

———. *Familiaris consortio*. In *Vatican Council II*, vol. 2, *More Post Conciliar Documents*, edited by Austin Flannery, 815–98. Northport, NY: Costello, 1998.

Morrisey, Francis G. "The Rights of Parents in the Education of Their Children (Canons 796–806)." *Studia Canonica* 23, no. 2 (1989) 429–44.

Pius XI, *Divini Illus Magistri*, http://www.vatican.va/holy_father/pius_xi/encyclicals/documents/hf_p-xi_enc_31121929_divini-illius-magistri_en.html.

Provost, James, H. "Title I: "The Obligations and Rights of All the Christian Faithful (cc. 134–159)." In *The Code of Canon Law: A Text and Commentary*, edited by James A. Coriden et al., 453–69. Mahwah, NJ: Paulist, 1985.

Sacred Congregation for Clergy (SCC). *Ad norman decreti*. In *Vatican Council II*, vol. 2, *More Post Conciliar Documents*, edited by Austin Flannery, 529–605. Northport, NY: Costello, 1998.

Sacred Congregation for the Doctrine of the Faith (SCDF). *Pastoralis Actio*. In *Vatican Council II*, vol. 2, *More Post Conciliar Documents*, edited by Austin Flannery, 103–15. Northport, NY: Costello, 1998.

United States Conference of Catholic Bishops (USCCB), *National Directory for Catechesis*. Washington, D.C: United States Conference of Catholic Bishops, 2005.

Vatican II Council. *Apostolicam Actuositatem*. In *Vatican Council II*, vol. 1, *The Conciliar and Post Conciliar Documents*, edited by Austin Flannery, 766–98. Northport, NY: Costello, 1998.

———. *Christus Dominus*. In *Vatican Council II*, vol. 1, *The Conciliar and Post Conciliar Documents*, edited by Austin Flannery, 564–90. Northport, NY: Costello, 1998.

———. *Gravissimum Educationis*. In *Vatican Council II*, vol. 1, *The Conciliar and Post Conciliar Documents*, edited by Austin Flannery, 725–37. Northport, NY: Costello, 1998.

———. *Lumen Gentium*. In *Vatican Council II*, vol. 1, *The Conciliar and Post Conciliar Documents*, edited by Austin Flannery, 350–426. Northport, NY: Costello, 1998.

5

Liturgical Catechesis and Catholic Identity

—Diana Dudoit Raiche

Introduction

ONCE TAKEN FOR GRANTED, the concept of Catholic identity has gained greater prominence since Vatican Council II. Not only is it a topic for social science research, but the findings of such research have also become of great interest to the church's leadership. Clergy and lay ecclesial ministers alike are interested in reliable sociological studies of changing currents and trends in the Catholic population because these serve as a barometer of the state of Catholic identity and can inform related pastoral decisions. Data trends deliver a wake-up call with clear implications, not just for the state of Catholic identity in general, but also for educational and catechetical initiatives that specifically aim at teaching the faith in ways that enhance Catholic identity.

For example, it had been hoped, or assumed, that immigrants would maintain cherished, culturally oriented faith practices even as they were assimilated into the North American cultural experience. However, new evidence from the Pew Research Center paints a different and sobering picture. Hispanic Catholic immigrants are not maintaining their Catholic identity once in the United Sates:

> About one-third of Mexicans (30 percent), Puerto Ricans (34 percent), Cubans (33 percent), Salvadorans (32 percent) and

Dominicans (34 percent) said they have switched from their childhood religion. About 5 percent of Hispanics, regardless of origin group, identify as mainline Protestant. But religious affiliations differ between Hispanic immigrants and those born in the United States. For example, the share of all Hispanic immigrants who are Catholic exceeds the rate among those born in the United States by 60 percent to 48 percent. Among Mexicans, 68 percent of immigrants identify as Catholic, compared with 51 percent of those born in the United States. Some 24 percent of Mexicans born in the U.S. said they are religiously unaffiliated, a rate about twice as high as among immigrants.[1]

An in-depth analysis of the reasons for such disaffections is beyond the scope of this chapter, but in a context of increased mobility and more porous cultural boundaries, it is understandable that it can be difficult to maintain the kind of Catholic identity associated with previous generations.

Another study from the Pew Research Center reveals that the Catholic Church in the US has been in decline for some forty years: "Over the past four decades, self-reported church attendance has declined among 'strong' Catholics as well as among Catholics overall. The share of all Catholics who say they attend Mass at least once a week has dropped from 47 percent in 1974 to 24 percent in 2012; among 'strong' Catholics, it has fallen more than 30 points, from 85 percent in 1974 to 53 percent last year."[2] Clearly, sociologists see Sunday Mass attendance as a key indicator of Catholic identity.

The decline in weekly attendance at Mass may also be evidence of the changing needs of modern-day Catholics, who require something more than programmatic catechesis to form and maintain Catholic identity. Notwithstanding the publication of the *Catechism of the Catholic Church* and the *United States Catholic Catechism for Adults,* both of which are intended to strengthen knowledge of the faith and therefore advance Catholic identity, evidence indicates that mere exposure to church teachings does not ensure a strong Catholic identity. Contemporary Catholics are influenced by alternative social relations, theories, and ideas that oftentimes differ from official church teaching. Some find it difficult to understand the reasons for church teachings. Georgetown theologian Peter Phan explains that "among Roman Catholics, it is not the case that there has been lacking a clear, insistent, repeated, definite, and definitive articulation of what Catholics must believe and practice. Rather it is the fact that, in spite of such articulation,

1. "Mexican and Dominican Catholics."
2. "'Strong' Catholic Identity."

some or even many of these teachings and practices, which the Magisterium regards as essential, do not, in the first place, appear to be convincing to the average Catholic."[3]

If such consistent direct teaching on its own does not engender strong Catholic identity in the current cultural context, then what does? The church points to the liturgy. In his 1998 apostolic letter *Dies Domini*, John Paul II makes clear that the significance of Sunday Mass attendance goes beyond mere obligation. "When its significance and implications are understood in their entirety," the document asserts, "Sunday in a way becomes a synthesis of the Christian life and a condition for living it well."[4] Sunday Mass attendance demonstrates faith in Jesus and that Catholic identity has taken root. Furthermore, faithfully attending Sunday liturgy demonstrates a commitment to ongoing formation in faith by living and praying as a disciple of Jesus Christ within a faith community. This synthesis of Christian life, as John Paul II describes Sunday Mass attendance, serves as a barometer for assessing Catholic identity. As the social science evidence shows, without a strong sense of Catholic identity, it is easier for some Catholics to separate themselves from the family of faith and the Sunday assembly.

A variety of recent church documents underscore this argument. For example, *Sacrosanctum Concilium* advances that "Sacraments . . . are signs . . . [which] belong in the realm of instruction. They presuppose faith, but by words and objects they also nourish, strengthen and express it."[5] Faith, which is a gift from God and the fruit of conversion to Jesus Christ, is necessary for Catholic identity, which is nourished through the sacraments. The *General Directory for Catechesis* (GDC) advances that liturgical formation is integrated in the pastoral care associated with authentic and effective catechesis for formation in faith.[6] The *National Directory for Catechesis* (NDC) reinforces this understanding by quoting *Catechesi tradendae*: "Catechesis is intrinsically linked with the whole of liturgical and sacramental activity."[7]

The *Rite of Christian Initiation of Adults* (RCIA) gives a sophisticated example of what the documents advance. Published in 2000, a report from the National Conference of Catholic Bishops (NCCB) shows that 64

---

3. Phan, "Religious Identity," 167–69.
4. John Paul II, *Dies Domini*, 81.
5. Vatican II, *Sacrosanctum Concilium*, 59.
6. Congregation for the Clergy, *General Directory for Catechesis* (GDC), 174.
7. United States Conference of Catholic Bishops, *National Directory for Catechesis* (NDC), 33.

percent of newly initiated Catholics who have gone through an authentic baptismal catechumenal process according to the RCIA attend Mass on a weekly basis.[8] Other data from The Catholic University of America sociologist William D'Antonio puts these numbers in context. In 1995 only 43 percent of adult Catholics were attending Sunday Mass, and by 2005 that number had dropped to 34 percent.[9] Even given the disparity of years when these surveys were conducted, it is evident that those formed in the faith through the baptismal catechumenate exhibit a stronger Catholic identity based on the indicator of Sunday Mass attendance. The 64 percent weekly attendance rate of new Catholics is nearly three times that of Catholics who were formed in the customary sacramental preparation system, ten percentage points higher than the rate reported by the Pew Research Center among "strong" Catholics in 2012, and 21 percentage points higher than the earlier 1995 D'Antonio data. The NCCB Report highlights that when properly implemented, the RCIA, which is both "a process of formation and a true school of faith,"[10] yields more positive Catholic identity based on Sunday Mass attendance.

It is instructive to reflect on the structure of formation that has yielded such robust Sunday Mass attendance. The baptismal catechumenate is a fruitful blend of instruction and formation in faith; it progresses through gradual stages; it unfolds the church's rites, symbols, and biblical signs; and it incorporates the catechumens into the Christian community of faith and worship.[11] The GDC names the process of formation in the baptismal catechumenate (RCIA) as the inspirational "model of its catechizing activity."[12] The GDC also advances that the baptismal catechumenate aims to achieve a "more integrated formation of the person rather than merely to communicate information. The restored catechumenate seeks to foster a committed conversion [to Jesus Christ] through a systematic catechesis based upon a more thorough integration of Sacred Scripture and Sacred Tradition, through liturgical catechesis, proper pastoring and insertion into the parish community."[13] The RCIA manifests a unique intersection of liturgy and catechesis in the restored baptismal catechumenate.

8. NCCB, *Journey to the Fullness of Life*, 56.
9. D'Antonio et al., *American Catholics Today*, 55.
10. United States Conference of Catholic Bishops, NDC, 35D.
11. Ibid.
12. Congregation for the Clergy, GDC, 90.
13. United States Conference of Catholic Bishops, NDC, 3.

This chapter addresses the problem of Catholic identity in relation to participation in liturgy as well as catechesis for and from liturgy. To explicate this relation, I begin by discussing the formation of identity and social processes associated with the church as a community of faith founded on the conversion to and love for Jesus Christ, which is expressed and lived out in its sacramental life.[14] I address this further by arguing that Catholic identity is necessarily contingent on the ongoing conversion of individuals, which initially begins and is supported by the social processes and structures of the RCIA process.[15] A central feature of the baptismal catechumenate (RCIA) vis-à-vis the formation of Catholic identity is liturgical catechesis, which is also relevant to the ongoing formation of Catholic identity among practicing Catholics. A key component of both liturgy and identity is its tie to the community. That is, I argue that personal identity as a Catholic is inextricably joined to the life of community and all of its social processes and structures. Finally, I describe the various components of the liturgical life of the church as it pertains to the formation of Catholic identity.

Identity and Identity in God through Christ

Identity Formation

Identity goes to the core of being human.[16] From a sociological perspective, Peter L. Berger and Thomas Luckmann claim identity is formed by social processes—that is, we *are* who we are *told* we are.[17] This social process, then, is a key element in subjective reality and stands in a dialectical relationship with society, which "exists as both objective and subjective reality." The three moments of the dialectical process (externalization, objectivation,

---

14. Sinwell, "Some Principles for Catechesis," 2.

15. Raiche, "Liturgical Catechesis."

16. The term identity is associated with sociological categories in which social processes both form and maintain one's subjective reality or "identity." Peter Steinfels advances that we should "stop thinking about Catholic identity as though this were something univocal.... There may be some overarching principles ... but there is no single way of embodying them, and it might be wiser to speak of Catholic identities in the plural." Steinfels, *A People Adrift*, 147–48. Peter Phan states that "[r]eligious identity is both personal and social; it is formed by meaning of oneself, others and the perception of others related to oneself." Phan, "Religious Identity and Belonging," 163–65.

17. Berger and Luckman, *The Social Construction of Reality: A Treatise in the Sociology of Knowledge*.

and internalization),[18] are operative whenever an "individual member of society . . . simultaneously externalizes his own being into the social world and internalizes it as an objective reality." For Berger and Luckmann, "to be in society is to participate in its dialectic."[19] Once formed, identity can be maintained, modified, or reshaped by subsequent social relations.[20]

The church itself is such a society, with its own social relations, social processes, and social structure. From a purely sociological perspective, the church has the constitutive elements needed to shape, form, maintain, and modify Catholic identity. Notwithstanding data that point to a changing dialectic in society, the church has formed Catholics with greater or lesser degrees of success in various expressions of Catholic identity for two thousand years.

From a faith formation perspective, theologian Rosemary Haughton proposes a theory of identity formation around the concept of communities that come together "on purpose."[21] She advances that it is a real decision of love that creates a real community.[22] A Christian community, founded on conversion to and love for Jesus Christ, is capable of influencing Christian identity because this love influences the way we identify with his life, death, and resurrection. Analyzing several types of Christian faith-based communities, she posits that people in love, or what she refers to as the first stages of conversion, tend to adopt behaviors that are not just possible, but

---

18. These three terms are specific to the analysis in Berger and Luckmann, *The Social Construction of Reality*. "As man externalizes himself, he constructs the world *into* which he externalizes himself. In the process of externalization, he projects his own meaning into reality. Symbolic universes, which proclaim that *all* reality is humanly meaningful and call upon the *entire* cosmos to signify the validity of human existence, constitute the farthest reaches of this projection" (104). Credit is given in note 80 here to Feuerbach, then, albeit in different directions, to Marx, Nietzsche, and Freud for developing the conception of projection. The process by which "the externalized products of human activity attain the character of objectivity is objectivation" (60). "Internalization is the immediate apprehension or interpretation of an objective event as expressing meaning, that is, as a manifestation of another's subjective processes which thereby becomes subjectively meaningful to myself" (129).

19. Ibid., 129. According to Berger and Luckmann, primary socialization occurs in childhood, leading to an internalization of the social order once identification occurs. Any subsequent process that inaugurates an individual into a new social context constitutes secondary socialization. Through the same process of internalization, society, identity, and reality are subjectively fixed.

20. Ibid., 173.

21. Haughton, *The Transformation of Man*, 153.

22. Ibid., 163.

"imperative, as the only adequate expression of their new self-awareness."[23] The theoretical implications for religious ritual and Catholic liturgy cannot be missed. For example, a community that is marked by "the community conversion event" as an occasion of transformation engages on purpose in something that has meaning. This meaning is deeper than can be fully expressed by mere doing. The community must draw upon ritual, the very function of which is to communicate deeper, more ineffable meaning, with or without words.[24]

Haughton's analysis of ritual also has implications for forming identity in a Catholic community. She contends, for example, that it is the ritual that "bridges the gap between formation and transformation."[25] In these bridging ritual events, there are those who come together to *be* converted, and the transformed-minded who come together because they *are* converted. Such a Christian community functions as an educational structure.[26] The error a transformed community can make with regard to identity formation is to attempt "to transfer the type of awareness, which is proper and inevitable in the context of transformation, wholly and untranslated into the formation context."[27] Without such translation, the transfer of awareness is just too much for those in the process of formation to receive. The gap exists because of the transformed community's lack of awareness of the relationship between formation and transformation.[28] Such a distinction is available only to those who have undergone the before, during, and after stages of the initial conversion experience. Future generations are not able to manifest the acquired behaviors of the converted who have had a primary, original experience of conversion, which is understood as falling in love with Jesus as a powerful "conversion event." When we understand our identity in Christ in this way, hearts, perspectives, and positions are capable of changing dramatically.[29]

Each individual in the community needs to undergo conversion, that is, the transformative experience that motivates the adoption of

23. Ibid., 184.
24. Ibid., 176.
25. Ibid., 177.
26. Ibid., 155.
27. Ibid., 185.
28. Ibid.
29. Haughton's description is consistent with the conversion associated with the baptismal catechumenate.

transformed behaviors. This is precisely what the RCIA intends and why the first stage of the catechumenate process, the period of evangelization and pre-catechumenate, is not dedicated to teaching doctrine to inquirers immediately. Rather, it relies on God's grace coupled with human effort to create the conditions for an inquirer to begin the conversion journey of turning to Christ through exposure to Scripture and social processes that mediate the Catholic Church's practices and traditions. The transformed community still has to contend with moral failings; that is, members of the community may fall away from the original conversion. These "deviations" do not necessarily mean that they did not experience conversion.[30] It may mean that the conditions for maintaining Catholic identity are inadequate or inaccessible after such a conversion experience. Identity of an individual or a group is usually understood in light of differences, well-defined boundaries, and an over-against stance in relation to other people's beliefs, ideas, and practices. However, Catholic identity in Christ aims at bringing us into communion with him as brothers and sisters in Christ, guided by boundaries informed by gospel imperatives and the ecclesial community.

Catholic Identity and Conversion

The identity of a baptized Catholic, in the order of grace, may be aided by the church as a society, according to a sociological perspective, or as a community of transformation, according to the perspective Haughton proposes. Regardless of how one seeks to account for it, the Catholic understanding of being human and identity formation is rooted in "an understanding of human existence . . . grounded in Jesus Christ as a revelation of the meaning of humanity in relation to God."[31] *Gaudium et Spes* (Pastoral Constitution on the Church in the Modern World) notes that "in reality it is only in the mystery of the Word made flesh that the mystery of humanity truly becomes clear."[32] This is the basis for the understanding that grace builds on nature.

---

30. Ibid., 205.

31. Scanlon, "Christian Anthropology," 27–28. Rom 6:3–11 evokes imagery of Christ's death for us and evokes a deeper understanding of our participation in Christ's death as we die to sin in the waters of baptism; John 3:3–38 evokes imagery of Christ's rising to new life as we become aware of our being regenerated in the waters of baptism.

32. Vatican II, *Gaudium et Spes*, 22.

The RCIA process of formation is thoroughly grounded in this understanding of Christian anthropology and the spiritual journey each individual takes to embrace Jesus as the Christ. The intersection and interplay between catechesis and liturgy in the RCIA provides a specific structure that facilitates one's spiritual journey and conversion to a new identity in Christ. The structure for catechesis in each of the four periods of formation in the RCIA (evangelization and pre-catechumenate; catechumenate; purification and enlightenment; and mystagogy) aims to bring about conversion to Jesus Christ through a gradual process that is punctuated by major and minor liturgical rites. These rites celebrate the various stages of the conversion process leading to full initiation into the church and incorporation into Jesus Christ through baptism. That is why the catechumenate is called a "school of faith and a process of formation"; it is a socially constructed process structured around catechesis connected to specific liturgical rites. A specific liturgical catechesis both precedes the celebration of a rite and follows the ritual celebration as a mystagogical reflection on multiple elements within the ritual.

Haughton would describe this process as newly baptized Catholics (neophytes) becoming part of the community of the transformed and eager to function within the transformation community. From Berger's and Luckmann's perspective, the RCIA structure of formation offers the requisite social processes, social relations, and social structures for identity formation. From the perspective of the sociological lexicon, RCIA employs both social relations and social processes that span the four periods of the catechumenate and work within a social structure of ritual celebrations in order to form, nurture, and maintain Catholic identity.

The guidelines governing the RCIA process explain how one's identity within the larger society of the church comes about in the structure of Christian initiation:

> In the sacraments of Christian initiation we are freed from the power of darkness and joined to Christ's death, burial and resurrection. We receive the Spirit of filial adoption and are part of the entire people of God in the celebration of the memorial of the Lord's death and resurrection. Baptism incorporates us into Christ and forms us into God's people . . . . By signing us with the gift of the Spirit, confirmation makes us more completely the image of the Lord and fills us with the Holy Spirit, so that we may bear witness to him before all the world and work to bring the Body of Christ to its fullness as soon as possible (*Ad Gentes*, no. 36).

Finally, coming to the table of the eucharist, we eat the flesh and drink the blood of the Son of Man so that we may have eternal life (See John 6:55) and show forth the unity of God's people. Thus the three sacraments of Christian Initiation closely combine to bring us, the faithful of Christ, to his full stature and to enable us to carry out the mission of the entire people of God in the Church and in the world. (*Lumen Gentium*, no. 31).[33]

The RCIA provides a theological structure that honors human identity, promotes identity in Christ, and accomplishes a complete catechesis and formation in faith that is both deductive and inductive. Such a Catholic identity is rooted in conversion. The fruit of this conversion, faith and identity in Christ, is greater than the sum of the individual elements of the RCIA.

Liturgical Catechesis in RCIA and Catholic Identity

Unique to and inherent in the RCIA process is liturgical catechesis, which is a distinct, "eminent" form of catechesis that "explains the contents of prayers" and the "meaning of signs and gestures" as it "educates to active participation, contemplation, and silence."[34] This description of liturgical catechesis is similar to the definition in the *Catechism of the Catholic Church*, which notes that liturgical catechesis "aims to initiate people into the mystery of Christ (It is a 'mystagogy.') by proceeding from the visible to the invisible, from the sign to the thing signified, from the 'sacraments' to the 'mysteries.'"[35] The NDC describes liturgical catechesis in the following way:

> Liturgical catechesis is most explicit in the form of the homily received during the celebration of the sacraments. As such, liturgical catechesis within the scope of a sacred action is an integral part of that action [SC, 35]. Its function is "the immediate preparation for reception of the different sacraments, the celebration of sacramentals and above all the participation of the faithful in the Eucharist as a primary means of education in faith" [GDC, 51]. Liturgical catechesis also includes reflection upon the ritual celebration.[36]

---

33. ICEL, *Rite of Christian Initiation of Adults*, xiv.
34. Congregation for the Clergy, GDC, 71.
35. Catholic Church, *Catechism of the Catholic Church*, 1075.
36. United States Conference of Catholic Bishops, NDC, 17C.

These characteristics of liturgical catechesis are constitutive of its inductive methodology, which the NDC states is necessary for the deductive, kerygmatic, or descending methodology to have full value.[37]

The final report from the Extraordinary Synod of Bishops in 1985 acknowledged that "catecheses must once again become paths leading into liturgical life (mystagogical catechesis), as was the case in the Church's beginnings."[38] For those schooled in the rituals and structure of the ancient catechumenate, such foundational catecheses are recognizable in the restored *Rite of Christian Initiation of Adults* (1972).[39]

Prior to the restoration of the ancient catechumenate, Benedictine scholar Virgil Michel edited *The Christ Life Series* (1934–35).[40] This series "provided a comprehensive and systematic introduction to the liturgical life of the church ... developed knowledge and awareness of liturgy as a vital component of Christian life ... and gave instruction on the history and meaning of the liturgical rites."[41] Michel was well equipped to edit such a new type of religion series, having been exposed to the liturgical movement and new currents in liturgical theology during his studies in Europe. Unfortunately, the experiment with this form of liturgical catechesis in the United States did not last. Mary Kay Oosdyke reflects on the situation by observing that while religious educators know liturgy is important to Christian life, they are not cognizant of the fact that liturgy teaches.[42] Keeping liturgy and catechesis in separate silos in a religious education context is counterproductive—for "the liturgy is the summit toward which the activity of the Church is directed; it is also the fount from which all her power flows."[43] It

---

37. Ibid., 29.

38. John Paul II, *Second Extraordinary Synod: Final Report*, 9.

39. *Sacrosanctum Concilium* called for the restoration of the catechumenate. The *Rite of Christian Initiation of Adults* was promulgated in Latin in 1972. It was translated into English in 1974. The current 1988 ritual text is an inculturated ritual for the Church of the United States.

40. Oosdyke, "Acquiring a Sense of Liturgy," 323–37. Oosdyke recounts the story of *The Christ Life Series* for elementary students. She describes it as "a unique religion series based in the theology of the liturgical movement" and concludes that the liturgical vision it promoted had relevance for the questions and problems being experienced in religious education in the United States in the 1980s.

41. Ibid., 330.

42. Ibid., 336.

43. United States Conference of Catholic Bishops, NDC, 33, quoting Vatican II, *Sacrosanctum Concilium*, 10. See also CCC, 1069.

is the "privileged place for catechizing the People of God."[44] Catechesis both precedes and springs from the liturgy; liturgy is therefore itself inherently catechetical.[45] Liturgy is a privileged, structured experience that forms us at the level of our identity, that is, at the core of our being. Peter Phan reminds us that this identity is formed by steeping oneself in the tradition, which includes beliefs, rituals, prayer, and ethical practice.[46]

Catholics are generally ill-prepared to recognize, explain, or appropriate the theology, ecclesiology, and sacramentality manifested in a particular liturgical celebration. While some may have a passing familiarity with the eucharistic prayers due to hearing the words or reading the printed text in a missal, most merely know the proper places in the liturgy for assembly responses, which is noteworthy. However, the deeply theological significance of ritual actions, silence, or music may elude many in the assembly. A consistently robust liturgical catechesis is essential for acquiring the language of liturgy, so that one is able to experience liturgy with "full, conscious, active participation"[47] and also apprehend its meaning.

There is good reason why the primacy of the patristic style of Catholic formation inherent in the baptismal catechumenate is a recurring theme in official church documents and directories. The RCIA manifests the intersection of liturgy and catechesis at its best, offering the opportunity for a "process of formation and true school of faith." RCIA consists of a family of rites structured to facilitate conversion, to form the whole person as a disciple of Jesus Christ, and to prepare one to manifest Catholic identity by living and practicing the faith and giving authentic Christian witness to the world.

Primacy of Liturgy: *Lex Orandi, Lex Credendi*—Foundations for Liturgical Catechesis

Lex orandi, lex credendi (loosely translated, "as the church prays, so the church believes") is an axiom that sums up liturgical theology.[48] The wisdom of the axiom is equally appropriate for those who undergo the rituals

---

44. Ibid., quoting CCC, 1074.
45. Ibid., 33.
46. Phan, "Religious Identity," 183.
47. Vatican II, *Sacrosanctum Concilium*, 14.
48. De Clerk, "*Lex orandi, lex credendi*," 178–200; and Irwin, *Liturgical Theology*, 11–17.

in the baptismal catechumenate and the faithful who participate in liturgy and sacraments regularly. It communicates that what we believe compels us to adopt certain practices and behaviors. Ritual celebration can matter greatly for our spiritual understanding and for the cultivation of our Catholic identity. Every ritual has the capacity to form, maintain, and modify us. Such formative work occurs within a community that inherently embodies human social relations, social process, and social structure.

Sometimes the liturgy draws us in; sometimes not so much. Liturgist Louis-Marie Chauvet explains why this is so by making observations about an aspect of liturgy he calls "symbolic break."[49] This term refers to intentional decisions that lead the assembly into another, non-utilitarian world so that there is room for God, room for effecting in our physical bodies—"through the arrangement of the place, the type of language and objects they use—what they say in the confession of faith."[50] Some examples of symbolic break include the following: sites exclusively dedicated to religious rituals (rather than ordinary locations like a parish hall); chalices made of precious metal (versus an ordinary goblet taken from the kitchen); and the use of ancient languages or distinctive repetitions (rather than using improvised or casual language).

Symbolic breaks are essential components of effective liturgical celebrations. However, it is important to strike a proper balance. When the symbolic breaks are overemphasized, liturgies can be rendered irrelevant and obscure to those who experience them. On the other hand, when there is not enough symbolic separation from ordinary life, liturgies can cease to convey anything of significance. Insufficient separation is the product of situating liturgy too close to everyday life, trivializing the language by "improvisation," avoiding clericalism by presiding without vesture, or ignoring the importance of the space for the rite, and so on. All of these things can become an "engagement in self-celebration under the cover of Jesus Christ to impose on 'God' its own ideology. When this happens, one is squarely on the wrong level."[51]

Examining recent catechetical practice, the GDC raises concerns about "a weak and fragmentary link with the liturgy," which manifests itself in limited attention to liturgical symbols and rites, scant use of the liturgical fonts, catechetical courses with little or no connection with the liturgical year, and

49. Chauvet, *The Sacraments*, 105.
50. Ibid., 103–6.
51. Ibid.

the marginalization of liturgical celebrations in catechetical programs."[52] Such manifestations may occur in both post-baptismal catechesis or in initiatory catechesis when the intended balance of deductive and inductive methods, inherent in the baptismal catechumenate, is ignored. When this occurs, it should not be surprising that Catholic identity is weakened. As we have seen in the NCCB report, when people in the catechumenate are exposed to proper liturgical catechesis, they attend Mass at higher rates.

While liturgical catechesis is a specific kind of catechesis, it pays attention to the overarching, universal catechetical tasks. The GDC enumerates six universal tasks in its presentation of a program for a complete catechesis: 1) knowledge of the faith; 2) knowledge of liturgy and sacraments; 3) knowledge of moral formation in Jesus Christ; 4) knowing how to pray with Christ; 5) knowing how to live in community and participate in the life and mission of the church; 6) knowing how to live with a missionary spirit, including how to be in dialogue with other religions.[53] These tasks "constitute a unified whole" and are intended to function so that "one aspect is not separated from the rest to the detriment of others."[54] This structured approach to catechesis is meant to guide all catechesis, including liturgical catechesis.

Knowledge of Scripture used at a particular liturgy, for example, aids knowledge of the faith. Understanding what is happening at a baptism during Sunday liturgy solidifies prior knowledge of liturgy and sacraments. Instruction and edification through a homily can influence moral formation and behavior. Praying the Our Father during liturgy immerses us in the prayer Jesus himself gave us and informs the nature of our relationships. Being present for liturgy teaches us how to become an assembly and part of a faith community. When firmly rooted in one's own tradition, one has the confidence to enter into meaningful dialogue rather than argue with others who are affiliated with another faith tradition. This makes the Christian witness, and therefore Catholic identity, all the more powerful, compelling, and believable.

Liturgical catechesis, then, imparts knowledge of the meaning of the liturgy and sacraments in a manner that puts people in touch with the mystery of faith at a deeper level. A deep commitment to Christ's paschal mystery inherent in the liturgy is essential for the formation of Catholic

---

52. Congregation for the Clergy, GDC, 30; John Paul II, "Apostolic Exhortation *Catechesi Tradendae*," 23.

53. United States Conference of Catholic Bishops, NDC, 20.

54. Ibid., 20.

identity. When Catholics walk away from the church and the sacraments (especially the Eucharist), it is possible that they were never truly formed in knowledge of and meaning of liturgy and the sacraments. The desire to know the content of the faith flows from the desire to be joined with Christ in the community prayer *par excellence*, eucharistic liturgy. An experience of God's love through Jesus compels us to live moral lives.[55]

The *Ecclesia* and Catechesis

All catechetical activity is rooted in the church, and therefore, the church directs those initiatives concerned with forming, maintaining, or modifying Catholic identity. The question then emerges, given that conversion happens and faith follows: Is there a stable "formation community" capable of creating a "community of the transformed"?[56] The gospel and the sacraments equip people to participate in the church's mission to proclaim Jesus and build the kingdom of God through works of social justice. But alternative social processes, social relations, and outside influences that gain traction can modify, diminish, or destroy a weakened Catholic identity when a Catholic is absent from the society of the church community, a Catholic school, or a catechetical formation program. When absent from these reinforcements, some Catholics may find it easier to disconnect not only from the church community at Sunday Mass, but also from church teaching, as social science data validates.

The *aggiornamento* inaugurated by Vatican Council II unwittingly dismantled some aspects of Catholic culture that had been the common means by which lay people expressed Catholic identity. Notwithstanding the philosophical and theological distinctiveness of Catholicism, Catholic identity was previously defined for many lay faithful by an over-against doctrinal position in relation to Protestants. It was also associated with certain pious disciplines, such as abstaining from meat every Friday, covering women's hair at Mass, and waiting in long lines for confession before Mass or on Saturday afternoons. When boundaries between ecclesial traditions softened and some traditional outward expressions of Catholicism disappeared, the average layperson wondered: What constitutes Catholic identity? Memorized answers from one of the several catechisms that were published in the United States prior to Vatican II did not necessarily help a

---

55. See United States Conference of Catholic Bishops, NDC, 33.
56. Haughton, *The Transformation of Man*, 180–241.

lay person navigate a rapidly changing social, cultural, religious, and liturgical landscape.

Peter Phan addresses this issue of Catholic identity in light of the role of religious educators, "whose task is to shape the religious identity of students."[57] He advances that while "theological reflections on catholicity are helpful and indeed profound and must be kept in mind as we discuss the issue of Catholic identity, they cannot be readily translated into a set of criteria to settle the question of who is Roman Catholic today."[58] First, allegedly distinctive Roman Catholic characteristics are not uniformly understood and are not evaluated using the same criteria. Second, Catholic identity is not the same as the "distinctiveness of Roman Catholicism," for identity is founded in what is universal and theological; the "distinctiveness of Roman Catholicism" relies on sociological and canonical criteria. Third, the already-baptized Catholic may not necessarily understand what church authorities and theologians posit as theological and canonical criteria for Catholic identity.[59]

Helpful to our understanding of Catholic identity is the following description of a Catholic Christian from *Lumen Gentium* (Dogmatic Constitution on the Church): "Fully incorporated into the Church are those who, possessing the Spirit of Christ, accept all the means of salvation given to the Church together with her entire organization, and who—by the bonds constituted by the profession of faith, the sacraments, ecclesiastical government, and communion—are joined in the visible structure of the Church of Christ, who rules here through the Supreme Pontiff and the bishops."[60] Of course, while being baptized constitutes a person in the church, a specifically initiatory and liturgical catechesis is required to facilitate a person's coming to understand and appropriate a true Catholic identity. According to *Lumen Gentium*:

> The one Mediator, Christ, established and constantly sustains here on earth his holy church, the community of faith, hope and charity, as a visible structure through whom he communicates truth and grace to everyone. But, the society equipped with hierarchical structures and the mystical body of Christ, the visible society and the spiritual community, the earthly church and the church

---

57. Phan, "To Be Catholic," 159.
58. Ibid., 163.
59. Ibid., 164.
60. Vatican II, *Lumen Gentium*, 14.

endowed with heavenly riches, are not to be thought of as two realities. On the contrary, they form one complex reality comprising a human and a divine element.[61]

Catholic identity, then, has divine and human roots. What is more, identity, including Catholic identity, has both personal and communal aspects. Without faith, there is no foundation for Catholic identity. Without a witnessing community, personal Catholic identity can be weakened. Without a connection to Christ through the eucharistic liturgy, both personal and communal Catholic identity may be weakened and destroyed. Conversely, Catholic identity flourishes when individuals and communities gather willingly Sunday-by-Sunday for the eucharistic liturgy.

Sustaining Catholic Identity through Liturgical Catechesis

In his encyclical *Fides et Ratio*, Pope John Paul II invokes the well-known admonition "know thyself." These words, inscribed on the temple portal at Delphi in Greece, set Socrates in search of truth; their quotation in the encyclical is the Pope's way of sending the message that the search for truth is a search for the self—that is, for identity.[62] The search for truth also invites us to delve more deeply into the eucharistic liturgy. It is our connection with the paschal mystery that puts human life into a proper context.[63] This life on earth is not a dress rehearsal with an option for a "do-over." It involves a journey to know who we are in God, to discover to whom we belong, to discover our ultimate purpose. Joining our lives with the life of Christ at liturgy is intended to be a transformative experience. In the entrance procession, for example, church-goers are expected to leave distractions and obstacles to faith at the church door so that each person can become united as an assembly at the celebration. Catholic identity, originating as it does from an intimate relationship with Jesus Christ through baptism, needs to be nurtured through celebrating the liturgy and the sacraments often and well, especially the Eucharist.

Liturgical catechesis is a method to advance understanding of how continual celebration of the sacraments is necessary to maintain identity in Christ. The tripartite method for liturgical catechesis involves preparing for

---

61. Ibid., 8, quoting Pius XII, *Mystici Corporis*, 221, and *Humani Generis*, 571.
62 McInerny, "Identity, Divine Filiation, and the Eucharist," 29.
63. See Catholic Church, *Catechism of the Catholic Church*, 1067.

liturgy, participating in its celebration, and reflecting on that celebration to advance an understanding of its meaning. In fact, liturgical catechesis follows the pattern of the liturgical year in a repeated pattern of preparation, celebration, and reflection with each particular liturgical celebration. In the season of Advent, for example, there is a period of time to prepare for the Christmas season that, far from being just a celebration of Christmas Day, helps us prolong the experience of the incarnation in the present moment. Following the Christmas season, we have the gift of Ordinary Time for reflecting on the meaning of what was celebrated.

Such a pattern is countercultural. Contemporary culture rewards rushing from one thing to the next, which has the effect of dulling our senses, rendering even the most glorious experience a fleeting memory, as we move on to the next big thing. Setting aside time to prepare for Christmas may be normative, but setting aside a period of time to reflect on Christmas, giving the mind and heart space to savor the experience, to enjoy insights, and to connect dots between and among elements of the liturgical season, is not. Yet such reflection is absolutely necessary if we are to see ourselves as God sees us, and if we are to grow in the search for truth that leads ultimately to Christ.

This method for liturgical catechesis can be applied not only to liturgical seasons, but to elements within a particular liturgy. In order for the full, active, and conscious liturgical participation promoted by liturgical catechesis to occur, one must have an acquaintance with the language of the liturgy in sign, symbol, gesture, word, and silence. The power of the liturgy to teach is highlighted in Pope John Paul II's apostolic letter *Mane Nobiscum Domine*, in which he calls for celebrating the liturgical signs well in order to bring about a deeper mystagogical understanding of their meaning.[64]

Sacrosanctum Concilium identifies constitutive elements of the liturgy that are the key elements also for liturgical catechesis. A close examination of that authoritative document reveals what has been in plain view and, yet, not fully appreciated. Paragraph 33 advances that "the visible signs used by the liturgy to signify invisible divine realities have been chosen by Christ or the church. Thus not only when things are read 'that were written for our instruction' (Rom 15:4), but also when the church prays or sings or acts, the faith of those taking part is nourished and their minds are raised to God, so that they may offer him their worship as intelligent beings and receive

---

64. John Paul II, *Mane Nobiscum Domine*, 17.

his grace more abundantly."⁶⁵ Notwithstanding the necessity of human cooperation with grace, it is important to recall that faith is God's gift in the order of grace. Therefore, it is necessary to consider how Catholic identity, which is the fruit of faith, is also not totally of our doing, engineered by mere human effort or tactics.

Focusing on ritual and prayers, *Sacrosanctum Concilium* gives a full program of instruction on how these elements can be incorporated in liturgical catechesis:

> Christ's faithful, when present at this mystery of faith, should not be there as strangers or silent spectators; on the contrary, through a good understanding of the rites and prayers they should take part in the sacred service conscious of what they are doing, with devotion and full involvement. They should be instructed by God's word and be nourished at the table of the Lord's body; they should give thanks to God; by offering the immaculate victim, not only through the hand of the priest, but also with him, they should learn to offer themselves as well; through Christ the Mediator, they should be formed day by day into an ever more perfect unity with God and with each other, so that finally God may be all in all.⁶⁶

Scripture forms an essential component in this regard: "Sacred Scripture is of the greatest importance in the celebration of the liturgy. For from it are drawn the lessons which are read and which are explained in the homily; from it too come the psalms which are sung. It is from scripture that the petitions, prayers and hymns draw their inspiration and their force, and that actions and signs derive their meaning."⁶⁷ Scripture, a source for liturgical prayer, is the inspired word of God; it is a narrative that is more than mere storytelling. Therefore, it is good to remember that the church defines catechesis as a ministry of the word of God.⁶⁸ The primacy of the word of God at liturgy is the topic of an in-depth study by sociologist Nancy Ammerman, in which she demonstrates that stories are a key vehicle for expressing and transmitting faith, and thus religious identity.⁶⁹

---

65. Vatican II, *Sacrosanctum Concilium*, 33.
66. Ibid., 48.
67. Ibid., 24.
68. United States Conference of Catholic Bishops, NDC, 18, quoting John Paul II, "Apostolic Exhortation *Catechesi Tradendae*," 27.
69. Winston, "Teach Your Children Well," 271.

Paragraph 27 of *Sacrosanctum Concilium* addresses the role of the community and sense of the church. "Whenever rites, according to their specific nature, make provision for communal celebration involving the presence and active participation of the faithful, it is to be stressed that this way of celebrating them is to be preferred, as far as possible, to a celebration that is individual and, so to speak, private."[70] The preceding paragraph notes how "liturgical services are not private functions, but are celebrations belonging to the church, which is the 'sacrament' of unity."[71] Catechizing on the meaning of community is founded in an experience of becoming an assembly around the eucharistic table. For this reason, the document places priority on ritual as being primarily communal.

Signs and symbols, which need to be interpreted, are constitutive of Catholic liturgical language and therefore are essential elements for liturgical catechesis. Paragraph 59 establishes a firm foundation:

> The purpose of the sacraments is to make people holy, to build up the Body of Christ and finally to give worship to God; but being signs they also have a teaching function. They not only presuppose faith, but by words and objects they also nourish, strengthen, and express it; that is why they are called "sacraments of faith." They do indeed impart grace, but, in addition, the very act of celebrating them disposes the faithful most effectively to receive this grace in a fruitful manner, to worship God rightly, and to practice charity. It is therefore of highest importance that the faithful should readily understand the sacramental signs and should with great eagerness frequent those sacraments that were instituted to nourish Christian life.[72]

The role of liturgical catechesis is to unpack meaning in the multitude of signs and symbols at liturgy. Since signs and symbols are part of the language of liturgy, knowing how to read this language contributes to the power of the liturgy to form, nurture, and maintain Catholic identity.

Music, gesture, and silence are also appropriate elements for liturgical catechesis, as evidenced in paragraph 112: "The musical tradition of the universal Church is a treasure of inestimable value, greater than that of any other art. The main reason for this preeminence is that, as a combination of sacred music and words, it forms a necessary or integral part of the solemn

---

70. Vatican II, *Sacrosanctum Concilium*, 27.
71. Ibid., 26.
72. Ibid., 59.

liturgy."[73] Singing and participation in acclamations, responses, psalmody, antiphons, actions, gestures, and bearing are constitutive elements of liturgical catechesis, along with reverent silence at the proper times.[74] These three elements, music, gesture, and silence, are the inductive means of communicating theological content without which deductive or didactic instruction is not complete.[75]

These paragraphs from *Sacrosanctum Concilium* name essential elements for liturgical catechesis: signs, prayers, scripture, community and sense of the church, symbols, music, and silence. They also clarify how each of these elements can function as content for liturgical catechesis. When one comprehends this lexicon at a deeper level, engages in the ritual actions they facilitate, and reflects on the content conveyed, Catholic identity is formed, maintained, and strengthened.

Conclusion

In response to evidence of decline in Catholic identity, social scientists and church theologians have turned more focused attention to the processes of identity formation and its maintenance. Knowing more about these processes can help arrest or even reverse the decline in Catholic identity, thereby strengthening the church. The liturgical rites and catechesis that are constitutive of the RCIA process are integral to this endeavor. Catechesis may be defined as formation in faith, a faith that is the fruit of conversion to Jesus Christ. Because the catechesis inherent in the catechumenate is held up as the model and inspiration for all forms of catechesis, it is important to acknowledge that it is a model structured around liturgies. Therefore, liturgy—Eucharist as well as other rituals that constitute the full complement of rites in the RCIA—becomes the focal point for examining and forming Catholic identity theologically, catechetically, and communally. The documents of the church make it abundantly clear that liturgy is the nexus and fulcrum around which Catholic identity revolves because our identity is in God through faith in Jesus Christ.

We are born as children of parents and also children of God. In baptism we become adopted heirs of the kingdom of God and thus begin a

---

73. Vatican II, *Sacrosanctum Concilium*, 112.

74. Ibid., 30.

75. United States Conference of Catholic Bishops, NDC, 29, quoting Congregation for the Clergy, GDC, 72.

life-long journey to comprehend and embrace that identity. In confirmation we receive the seal of the Holy Spirit to strengthen us for this journey. In Eucharist we receive the real presence of Christ as food for the journey. Jesus, who is our brother, is also our redeemer. The church, like a mother, offers shelter, instruction, and formation. The community that gathers in faith in Jesus's name becomes a formation community to assist in shaping our Catholic identity. As human beings, we have only one choice: to develop and to grow into our true identity step by step, decision by decision. The alternative is to wander aimlessly in the desert, distracted and complaining. Gathering together from age to age around the table of the Lord is how Catholic identity is formed, maintained, and more completely realized. Liturgical catechesis is the method that helps us understand, to the extent we can, the life-giving language of liturgy.

Bibliography

Berger, Peter L., and Thomas Luckman. *The Social Construction of Reality: A Treatise in the Sociology of Knowledge*. Garden City, New York: Anchor Books Doubleday, 1967.

Catholic Church. *Catechism of the Catholic Church*. Washington, DC: United States Catholic Conference, 1994.

Chauvet, Louis-Marie. *The Sacraments: The Word of God at the Mercy of the Body*. Collegeville, MN: Liturgical, 2001.

Congregation for the Clergy. *General Directory for Catechesis* (GDC). Washington, DC: United States Catholic Conference, 1997.

D'Antonio, William V., et al. *American Catholics Today*. Latham, MD: Rowman and Littlefield, 2007.

De Clerk, Paul. "Lex orandi, lex credendi: The Original Sense and Historical Avatars of an Equivocal Adage." Translated by Thomas M. Winger. *Studia Liturgica* 24 (1994) 178–200.

Haughton, Rosemary. *The Transformation of Man: A Study of Conversion and Community*. Springfield, IL: Templegate, 1967, 1980.

International Commission on English in the Liturgy (ICEL). *Rite of Christian Initiation of Adults*. Chicago: Liturgy Training Publications, 1988.

John Paul II. "Apostolic Exhortation *Catechesi Tradendae* (16 October 1979)." In *The Catechetical Documents: A Parish Resource*, 375–416. Chicago: Liturgy Training Publications, 1996.

———. *Dies Domini: On Keeping the Lord's Day Holy*. Boston, MA: Pauline, 1998.

———. *Mane Nobiscum Domine*. http://w2.vatican.va/content/john-paul-ii/en/apost_letters/2004/documents/hf_jp-ii_apl_20041008_mane-nobiscum-domine.

———. *Second Extraordinary Synod: Final Report*. http://www.vatican.va/news_services/press/documentazione/documents/sinodo_indice_en.html.

McInerny, Daniel. "Identity, Divine Filiation, and the Eucharist." *Assembly: A Journal of Liturgical Theology* (March 2009) 29–32.

"Mexican and Dominican Catholics Beat Out other Hispanic populations," *CathNews USA*, May 28, 2014. http://www.cathnewsusa.com/2014/05/mexican-dominican-catholics-beat-hispanic-populations/?newsletter=1.

National Conference of Catholic Bishops (NCCB). *Journey to the Fullness of Life: A Report on the Implementation of the Rite of Christian Initiation of Adults in the United States*. Washington, DC: United States Catholic Conference, 2000.

"'Strong' Catholic Identity at a Four-Decade Low in U.S." *Pew Research Center: Religion & Public Life*, March 13, 2013. http://www.pewforum.org/2013/03/13/strong-catholic-identity-at-a-four-decade-low-in-us/.

Oosdyke, Mary Kay. "Acquiring a Sense of Liturgy in Contemporary Times." *Religious Education* 84/3 (Summer 1989) 323–37.

Phan, Peter. "Religious Identity and Belonging Amidst Diversity and Pluralism: Challenges and Opportunities for Church and Theology." In *Passing on the Faith: Transforming Traditions for the Next Generation of Jews, Christians, and Muslims*, edited by James Heft, 162–84. New York: Fordham University Press, 2006.

———. "To Be Catholic or Not to Be: Is It Still the Question? Catholic Identity and Religious Education Today." *Horizons: Journal of the College Theology Society* 25/2 (1998) 159–80.

Raiche, Diana Dudoit. "Liturgical Catechesis as an Essential Dimension of Initiatory Catechesis in the *Rite of Christian Initiation of Adults* Adapted for Children." PhD dissertation, The Catholic University of America, 2011.

Scanlon, Michael J. "Christian Anthropology." In *The New Dictionary of Theology*, edited by Joseph A. Komonchak et al., 27–41. Collegeville, MN: Liturgical, 1987.

Sinwell, Joseph. "Some Principles for Catechesis from the Baptismal Catechumenate." In *Baptismal Catechumenate: An Inspiration for All Catechesis*, 1–5. Washington, DC: National Catholic Educational Association, 2002.

Steinfels, Peter. *A People Adrift: The Crisis of the Roman Catholic Church in America*. New York: Simon & Schuster, 2003.

United States Conference of Catholic Bishops. *National Directory for Catechesis* (NDC). Washington, DC: United States Conference of Catholic Bishops, 2005.

Vatican II Council. *Gaudium et Spes*. In *Vatican Council II*, vol. 1, *The Conciliar and Post Conciliar Documents*, edited by Austin Flannery, 903–1001. Northport, NY: Costello, 1996.

———. *Lumen Gentium*. In *Vatican Council II*, vol. 1, *The Conciliar and Post Conciliar Documents*, edited by Austin Flannery, 350–426. Northport, NY: Costello, 1996.

———. *Sacrosanctum Concilium*. In *Vatican Council II*, vol. 1, *The Conciliar and Post Conciliar Documents*, edited by Austin Flannery, 1–36. Northport, NY: Costello, 1996.

Winston, Diane. "Teach Your Children Well: Closing Observations on Constructing Religious Identity in the Next Generation." In *Passing on the Faith: Transforming Traditions for the Next Generation of Jews, Christians, and Muslims*, edited by James L. Heft, S.M., 264–74. New York: Fordham University Press, 2006.

6

Catholic Identity and Adult Moral Formation

—Fr. Mark O'Keefe, OSB

Introduction

CATHOLIC MORAL TEACHING IN the United States is in trouble. One research study after another tells us that self-identified Catholics hold largely the same moral beliefs as their fellow Americans, regardless of the presence of clear contrary moral teaching by the official teachers of the church. The 2006–08 Gallup Values and Beliefs Poll, for example, reveals that American Catholics are as "liberal"—or more so—than their non-Catholic counterparts on eight contemporary moral issues raised by the pollsters.[1] When asked about the acceptability of the following moral issues, Catholics and non-Catholics responded in this way:

"Moral acceptability" of the following:	Catholics	Non-Catholics
Abortion	40%	41%
Death penalty	61	68
Sex between an unmarried man and woman	67	57
Divorce	71	66

1. Newport, "Catholics Similar to Mainstream."

"Moral acceptability" of the following:	Catholics	Non-Catholics
Medical research using embryonic stem cells	63 %	62 %
Gambling	72	59
Homosexual relations	54	45

[Data adapted from 2006–08 Gallup Values and Beliefs Poll]

Note that the answers of Catholic respondents were virtually the same as non-Catholics on the questions of abortion and embryonic stem cell research. Even more noteworthy is the fact that, despite clear Catholic teaching against these practices, the Catholic respondents were actually more accepting than their non-Catholic counterparts of sex outside of marriage, divorce (and remarriage?), and homosexual relationships.

The lack of adherence of American Catholics in regard to these specific moral issues is consistent with a deeper problem of a more general decline in their acceptance of the moral authority of official church teaching. Contemporary research shows us that American Catholics are increasingly inclined to view themselves as their own arbiters of right and wrong.[2]

Consistent with a number of other studies, the Gallup poll mentioned above found that there is a significant difference in viewpoint between those Catholics who regularly attend Sunday Mass and those who do not. Only 24 percent of Catholics who regularly attend Mass, for example, view abortion as morally acceptable, compared to 52 percent of those who do not. Fifty-three percent of regularly church-going Catholics view sex

---

2. The 2001 study of Dean Hoge and his colleagues, for example, found that 71 percent of all non-Latino Catholics, 20–39 years of age, agreed with statement: "In the realm of morality, the final authority about good and bad is the individual's informed conscience" (Dean R. Hoge et al., *Young Adult Catholics*, 61). This statement could certainly be read as consistent with the long-standing Catholic moral tradition on the centrality of the informed conscience at the moment of choice, though it seems doubtful that a majority of the respondents were aware of the nuances of the traditional insistence on the necessary relationship of conscience with objective norms. This doubt is supported by a 2013 study of American Catholics by William V. D'Antonio and his colleagues who found that a majority of Catholic respondents believed that the individual alone—rather than either church leaders alone or church leaders and individuals in partnership—should be the final moral arbiter in questions of sexual and reproductive morality (66 percent for contraception, 57 percent for homosexual activity, 53 percent for nonmarital sex, and 52 percent for abortion). William V. D'Antonio et al., *American Catholics in Transition*, 75–76.

between unmarried persons as acceptable compared to 77 percent of their occasional Mass-attending counterparts. Forty-four percent of those who attend Mass regularly view homosexual relations as acceptable compared to 61 percent. Clearly, continued participation in the life of the church makes a significant difference in moral outlook. Based on their 2013 study of American Catholics, William D'Antonio and his colleagues conclude:

> Commitment to the Church had the strongest, most direct, and most consistent effect on the beliefs and practices we had studied. The more committed a Catholic was to the Church, the more likely he or she was to embrace Church teachings. The less committed one was to the Church, the more one was inclined toward beliefs and practices that did not conform to Church norms.[3]

Unfortunately, at the very same time, recent research has consistently shown that regular Mass attendance by Catholics is declining steadily.[4] Moreover, it cannot be ignored that even the regular church-goers in all of these recent studies do not express anything approaching universal acceptance of the church's official moral teaching. Mass attendance is a factor and an element in adherence to the church's moral and doctrinal teaching—and perhaps part of a strategy for gaining greater adherence—but it alone is not the answer.

In this chapter, we want to consider the challenge of adult Catholic moral formation in light of the reality revealed to us by recent social scientific research. How are bishops, pastors, and lay religious educators to form adult Catholics in accord with the moral wisdom of the Catholic

---

3. D'Antonio et al., *American Catholics in Transition*, 6–7. A 2008 study by the Center for Applied Research in the Apostolate (CARA), commissioned by the US Catholic Bishops, concurs: "In general, the more frequently one attends Mass, the more frequently he or she participates in other Church or religious activities, the greater his or her knowledge about the Catholic faith, the greater his or her awareness of current events in the Church, and the greater his or her adherence to Church teachings." CARA, *Sacraments Today*, 2.

4. The relevance of attending to correlation of active participation and adherence to church teaching is highlighted by declining percentages of Catholics who attend Mass regularly. D'Antonio and his colleagues have done five surveys of American Catholics between 1987 and 2011, and they found that while 44 percent of Catholics attended Mass weekly in 1987, only 31 percent did so in 2011. Since the most faithful church-goers are among the older, pre-Vatican II generation, and these Catholics are dying off, D'Antonio and colleagues foresee a likely continued decline in Mass attendance. D'Antonio et al., *American Catholics in Transition*, 22. The 2008 CARA study found that while 31.4 percent of Catholics are attending Mass on any given weekend, in fact, only 23 percent are attending Mass every week. CARA, *Sacraments Today*, 3.

Church and its tradition in contemporary American culture? Clearly, such formation is not simply a matter of clearer or more insistent reiteration of the church's teaching. Considering the Gallup research, for example, it seems unlikely that the church's position against abortion and homosexual relations was not clear to the Catholic respondents of the survey instrument. Embryonic stem cell research may be both too recent and too complex for many Catholics to be aware of the church's official opposition, but surely the same cannot be said about the morality of abortion or homosexual relations.

A fundamental challenge today for any moral formation or dialogue is the reality of widespread subjectivism in our culture.[5] Most contemporary Americans simply do not view morality as objective—that is, that there is an objective standard by which people might judge their actions and the actions of others as right or wrong. In our society, there is no objective measure of morality that is independent of each person's personal, subjective opinion or viewpoint. As research shows, even today's American Catholics tend to view each person as the arbiter of right or wrong for himself or herself. The modern Catholic moral tradition and official moral teaching, on the other hand, are grounded on the belief that there is a natural law that is morally binding and knowable, at least to some degree, by all human persons. Norms or rules drawn from the natural law, guided by the church's official teachers, are believed to be objectively true, regardless of individual knowledge of or opinions about them. Handing on the church's objective teaching in a society that does not accept the foundation of its claim to objectivity, and therefore its application to all persons, is a major difficulty today.[6] From the perspective of subjectivism, the objective moral teaching

---

5. In this context, the word "subjectivism" is being used in a popular sense, roughly equivalent to "relativism," to mean the belief that norms of human conduct are determined by each individual for himself or herself. It is opposed to the view that underlies Catholic moral teaching that there are objective norms of conduct—whether derived from the natural law or from Scripture—which reflect what is truly good for persons, whether or not individuals recognize or accept those norms. Thus, from the perspective of the Catholic moral tradition, it is possible to say that abortion is always wrong whether people accept that norm or not. This does not yet answer the question of personal guilt or sin, which takes into account more personal and situational considerations such as conscience and knowledge or ignorance of the objective good. Subjectivism, on the other hand, would view the morality of abortion as entirely dependent on each individual's personal assessment, independent of any objective standard or consideration.

6. We cannot engage, in this context, the subjective (as distinct from subjectivist) elements of Catholic morality, notably the individual conscience in its interaction with objective norms. Nor can we engage the question of legitimate disagreement or

of the Catholic Church can only appear as the effort to impose one distinctive, "merely" religious viewpoint on the moral lives of others. Thus, the question: How should the church carry on the work of adult moral formation in today's American culture?

This chapter will propose a response to that question first by focusing on the meaning and the contemporary reality of Catholic identity and commitment. The fact that regular church-going Catholics adhere more readily to the church's moral teaching already suggests that part of the response must involve strengthening Catholic identity and active participation. Based on some of the more encouraging news revealed by recent research and on recommendations offered by some of the researchers themselves, we will propose some avenues for bolstering Catholic identity and thereby fostering moral formation. In the end, it will be clear that adult Catholic moral formation today is closely linked with the challenge of the New Evangelization. Taking a distinct but related perspective, the contemporary focus on virtues in Christian ethics, in general, and in Catholic moral theology, in particular, will provide another lens for examining the importance of Christian self-identity in community and for achieving an effective adult Catholic moral formation. Finally—grounded in the current cultural realities, the recommendations already considered, and contemporary emphases in Catholic moral theology—we will propose the need for a broader vision of adult moral formation.

In what follows, then, we will be reviewing recent social scientific research as well as analyses and proposals offered by moral theologians and bishops. But surely the data and analyses merely confirm what parish ministers and religious educators encounter each day in ministry: So many Catholics who seem to be only marginally committed to the life of the church, who draw little of their self-identity and priorities from their faith, who do not appear to have much of a sense of why they continue to belong, and who therefore seem to wander in and out, pick and choose, are in danger of drifting away without much reflection. As a moral theologian, I began this reflection by saying "Catholic moral teaching in the United States is in trouble." But as a recent pastor, I know that the problem and the challenge are deeper and broader. They are profoundly pastoral. What is at

---

dissent from the church's teaching based on careful study, consultation, and prayer. For our purposes, perhaps it is not too much to assume that the majority of the Catholic respondents to the Gallup survey and other studies have not engaged in the careful discernment which, from a traditional Catholic perspective, might make such disagreement legitimate.

stake is the future of the Catholic faith and the shape of the Catholic Church in the United States. We have no reason to doubt the presence and working of the Holy Spirit. At the same time, we have every reason to study and reflect on the situation and to ponder ways to offer an effective response.

Catholic Identity in Contemporary American Culture

What is Catholic identity? Sociologist Dean Hoge and his colleagues suggest that this question can be examined both from the point of view of the *felt* identity of individuals as well as from the perspective of their actual adherence to identity-related characteristics of being Catholic and to subsequent behavior.[7] We will discuss this distinction in what follows from the perspective of felt *identity* and levels of actual *commitment*.

From the perspective of felt identity, social psychologists have discovered that a person's self-identity and self-concept depend on various elements (e.g., gender, race, ethnic background, physical characteristics, religious affiliation, hobbies and interests, career and achievements). We form our self-understanding from this variety of elements, which is unique to each of us. At the same time, self-concept also depends on how these various elements are prioritized, coordinated, and integrated by the individual. More specifically, then, an individual's Catholic identity involves the inclusion of "being Catholic" as an element by which the person understands him/herself. Further, it is the relative priority, centrality, or importance of "being Catholic" among the various other elements that make up the person's self-concept that determines if the self-identified Catholic is an active, conscious, and adherent Catholic or a more casual one. In this sense, we can say that persons have a strongly felt Catholic identity when they understand "being Catholic" to be central to their own self-concept relative, for example, to career goals and past achievements.

It is interesting and important to note that Catholics today can, at one and the same time, affirm their Catholicity, even while their beliefs and practices are not in keeping with what might traditionally count as criteria for being Catholic. On the one hand, D'Antonio and his colleagues found that 77 percent of US Catholics say that the Catholic Church is important to their lives, at least at some level; 88 percent say that it is unlikely that they would ever leave (with 56 percent saying that they would never leave); 75 percent say that "being Catholic is an important part of who I am; 68

---

7. Hoge et al., *Young Adult Catholics*, 174–80.

percent say "I can't imagine being anything but Catholic."[8] Likewise, the 2008 CARA study found that 77 percent of Catholics agree with the statement: "I am proud to be Catholic" (and 56 percent *strongly* agree), and 81 percent consider their Catholic faith to be important to their daily lives.[9] Similarly, ten years earlier, Hoge and his colleagues found that 95 percent of young adult Catholics wanted their children to receive religious instruction; 91 percent of non-Latino young Catholics who had children had had them baptized; and 72 percent of the same group had their children enrolled in some form of formal religious education.[10]

On the other hand, and at the same time, we have already noted the fact of seriously declining Mass attendance (although 84 percent of Catholics report that the Mass is personally meaningful to them[11]), lack of adherence to significant moral teaching, and increasing tendencies to ignore the church's moral authority in relation to individual moral judgment of right and wrong. But more, 78 percent of Catholics now believe that someone can be a good Catholic without attending weekly Mass, and 31 percent believe that someone can be a good Catholic without believing in the resurrection of Jesus.[12] Subjective feelings of attachment notwithstanding, Hoge summarizes the state of "being Catholic" among the young adult Catholics that he and others have studied:

> Their knowledge of the faith and of its traditional symbols and root metaphors is limited, fragmentary, or non-existent. Many seem to have lost much of the core narrative of the tradition and to have little connectedness with Catholic institutional life. As a consequence, young adult Catholics have a difficult time articulating a coherent sense of Catholic identity and expressing Catholicism's distinctiveness. . . . As the boundaries of Catholicism become weaker and more diffuse, preserving and transmitting the tradition's norms become more difficult.[13]

---

8. D'Antonio et al., *American Catholics in Transition*, 52.

9. CARA, *Sacraments Today*, 8.

10. Hoge et al., *Young Adult Catholics*, 58.

11. D'Antonio, *American Catholics in Transition*, 53. The 2008 CARA study found that 68 percent of American Catholics agreed with the statement that one could be a good Catholic without attending weekly Mass (4). Of this phenomenon, Hoge concludes: ". . . the Mass remains a primary source of institutional-based spiritual nurturance for young Catholics even while attendance rates have declined in recent decades" (167).

12. D'Antonio et al., *American Catholics in Transition*, 50.

13. Hoge et al., *Young Adult Catholics*, 16.

Hoge and his colleagues conclude that young adult Catholics hold together their appreciation of being Catholic with their lack of participation and adherence because they now construct "being Catholic" on their own terms. No wonder, then, that they see no compelling reason to leave the church despite their lack of adherence since they define what it means to be Catholic according to their own terms.[14] In spite of affirmations about liking to be Catholic in terms of feeling and preference, "it matters less to large numbers of young adults if they are Catholic in any institutional or communal sense."[15] This situation, says Hoge, is a sign of the "waning centrality" of young adults' Catholic identity:

> One of the most problematic trends among young adults is the decline in the perceived importance of being Catholic. Studies consistently show that the salience of Catholic identity has steadily waned. *Fewer young Catholics believe that it is important to be Catholic* [emphasis in original]. Many have developed a loose commitment to a vague "cultural Catholicism" or have espoused a more generic Christian lifestyle. Some have simply reduced their religious identity to being a good person.[16]

Types of Catholicism

Based on their research, Hoge and his colleagues speak of three types of Catholic identity among young adult Catholics (aged 20–39 in 2001).[17] "Parish Catholics" are those for whom being Catholic is central and important to their self-understanding. They tend to be church-going, accepting of church authority, and find meaning in their participation in parish life. "Spiritual Catholics" also view being Catholic as important and even central, but they are not active participants in the life of the parish or church except on special occasions. They are committed to some Catholic teachings and traditions but not to the institutional church. The third group, "contingent Catholics" (or "Christmas and Easter Catholics"), continue to view themselves as Catholics and intend to remain so, but their identity as Catholics is not central to their self-concept. Being Catholic is subordinated

14. Ibid., 226.
15. Ibid., 223.
16. Ibid., 17.
17. Ibid., 180–81.

to other elements of their identity and thus their focus, time, and energy are directed elsewhere.

D'Antonio and his colleagues have conducted five surveys of American Catholics since 1987. Not unlike Hoge and his associates, they distinguish Catholic identity from actual commitment to the church, and it is commitment that is the actual predictor of adherence to Catholic belief and practice. Together with a review of similar research, they conclude that Catholic *identity* is relatively stable while the level of church *commitment* by US Catholics is in a "slow decline."[18] The generation of pre-Vatican-II Catholics is dying, and it is this group that is most committed and adherent.[19] D'Antonio and colleagues suggest that 19 percent of today's American Catholics could be considered "highly committed" (down from 27 percent in 1987), 66 percent "moderately committed," and 14 percent with "low levels of commitment."[20] Forty-one percent of pre-Vatican-II Catholics (aged 71 or older in 2012) are highly committed (though, again, this generation is quickly dwindling); 20 percent of Vatican-II Catholics (aged 32-50 in 2012) are highly committed; and only 16 percent of younger Catholics belong to this group.

To conclude this section, it should be noted that not all of the findings of recent research are negative. We have already pointed to some hopeful aspects. The 2013 D'Antonio study found that a clear majority of contemporary Catholics say that being Catholic is somehow important to their lives (77 percent), are unlikely to leave the church (88 percent), cannot imagine being anything but Catholic (68 percent), and think that it is important for younger generations to grow up Catholic (75 percent).[21] Further, the 2008 CARA study likewise found that American Catholics report being proud of being Catholic (77 percent), consider their Catholic faith to be important to their daily life (81 percent), and consider themselves to be practicing Catholics (55 percent).[22] Sixty-one percent of Catholics agree that the sacraments are somehow essential to their faith.[23] However, we have already

18. D'Antonio et al., *American Catholics in Transition*, 8–9.

19. Ibid., 21.

20. For their study, D'Antonio and colleagues categorized as "highly committed," those US Catholics who indicated that the church was "most important" or "among the most important" parts of their lives, who attend Mass weekly, and who indicated that it was at least "very unlikely" that they would ever leave the Catholic Church. Ibid., 57.

21. Ibid., 52.

22. CARA, *Sacraments Today*, 8.

23 Ibid., 2.

seen that data like this co-exists with decreases in active participation in the life of the church and in adherence to Catholic doctrine, but we cannot ignore that there remains a base from which to build a more effective response to the situation.

Fostering the Centrality of Catholic Identity

Clearly the contemporary challenge of adult moral formation is linked with the work of strengthening a sense of Catholic identity, its centrality, and commitment to it. More than a decade ago, moral theologian Timothy O'Connell, in an innovative study of effective moral formation (or "making disciples," as he refers to such formation) in light of social scientific research, offers us some important insights.[24] Focusing on recent research concerning the values by which people actually live their lives, O'Connell argues that the task of moral formation of self-identified Catholics is not so much to convince them that certain activities or objectives (e.g., the protection of human life, attending to the poor, or attending Mass) are values. Rather, the challenge is to help them to come to see these values as central, relative to other things that they see as important. He concludes that "the project of moral formation, the making of disciples, is a project not of 'value-affirmation creation' but of 'value-preference modification'!"[25]

In regard to Catholic commitment, the challenge is not so much to get "being Catholic" on people's radar screens—that is, as an element of their self-identity—but rather to encourage it to become more central, a priority. Even the most marginal Catholic, for example, is likely to see church-going as a value. He or she may simply not see it as a high priority in light of other values. The problem is not that "Christmas and Easter" Catholics don't view "being Catholic" as a value; they just do not see it as a central value in regard to their choices about their actual priorities and activities. O'Connell argues that the goal is not the elimination of other values but re-ordering their preference.

Further, again based on social scientific research, O'Connell argues that value preferences are not simply a matter of individual decision or choice. Rather, such preferences are influenced by and indeed transmitted by the groups to which people belong. This transmission is not simply conceptual and rational. It is also importantly emotional, tied to the sense

24. O'Connell, *Making Disciples*.
25 Ibid., 60.

of belonging and the identity that goes with it. People embrace values, their ordering, and subsequent behaviors from the group-belonging, which is central to their identity. O'Connell concludes: "It is the group, then, that is the home of values. And if this is true, then making disciples may really be a process of creating communities of discipleship, homes where the value priorities of the disciple flourish."[26]

Within the groups to which we belong and that transmit values and value-preferences, we form significant, defining relationships. Our self-identity is critically formed, at a number of different levels, in the context of such relationships. The more numerous and the more personally significant these relationships in regard to one's self-identity, the more committed the person will be to that identity. The deeper the commitment to a self-identity, the more the person will embrace the associated group's value preferences and related behavioral expectations. Moral formation, O'Connell concludes, is really a matter of fostering relationships in a group within which identity—and especially identity centrality and commitment—are formed and maintained.[27]

Within groups and relationships, the individual's values, identity, and behavioral expectations are conveyed not so much by formal teaching and rational acceptance but by embracing and identifying with key narratives. Stories engage our imagination—visions of reality, of relationships, of identity, and of what is truly valuable. This is most obvious in children who learn what matters and how they should be and act through the fables, stories, and myths of heroes and heroines that they are told and thus imagined. More importantly, we might also say that they learn what they should value and how they should live through the living narrative of their parents' lives and the lives of other significant people.

The church, too, is importantly a community of formative narratives—for example, in the Scriptures, the lives of the saints, and the living example of Christians. But today fewer adult Catholics are participating in the life of the community in which those foundational stories can be transmitted. Fewer Catholic parents are taking their children to Mass where those stories are proclaimed, broken open, celebrated, and ritually enacted. The formative narratives for Catholics today are often coming instead from other, often antithetical groups. O'Connell argues that we are witnessing today the "centralizing of story-telling"—that is, the stories that we hear

26. Ibid., 85–86.
27. Ibid., 99.

and engage have become more and more the narratives that are told to us by secular, for-profit, corporate bodies through the media and advertising. Authentic Christian moral formation requires the effective re-telling of the Christian story—scriptural narratives, the lives of saints, the lived narrative of Christian disciples.[28]

We have not done justice to O'Connell's fine study, nor can we fully unfold the subsequent strategies that he suggests for effective and authentic moral formation ("making disciples"). For present purposes, we note that his proposal ultimately focuses on three key activities: religious education, liturgical worship, and parish life.[29] Interestingly, Hoge and his associates, in their 2001 study of young adult Catholics, offer similar recommendations in response to the problem of declining Catholic identity and commitment (and implicitly the contemporary challenge of adult moral formation):

> We heard from young adults that the experience of the liturgy, when attended by good homilies and good music, and by a strong and vibrant sense of community, keeps them connected to the Church and facilitates their return to it. It reinforces Catholicism's communal character and highlights the Eucharist as a sacramental source of spiritual life. . . . Conversely, where parish liturgy is experienced as 'boring,' 'mechanical,' and 'unwelcoming,' the effect is detrimental.[30]

Further, research found that those young Catholics who left the church for a time returned precisely because of perceived personal spiritual needs that they came to feel could be met by the church.[31] This is to say that contemporary men and women experience a spiritual yearning; and, when they can find tools for a response to this yearning in the church, they return to it.

Hoge and his colleagues offer ten recommendations to respond to the decline in Catholic identity and commitment among young adult Catholics.[32] Because of the clear linkage between identity/commitment and adherence to moral teaching, these recommendations are also relevant to adult moral formation. Among these recommendations are attention to the quality and style of liturgical celebration, the building up of an inviting parish community life, better adult religious education that speaks to

28. Ibid., 116–27.
29. Ibid., 141.
30. Hoge et al., *Young Adult Catholics*, 161.
31. Ibid., 166.
32. Ibid., 231–37.

contemporary Americans, and offering formation in spirituality and prayer that responds to the aspirations and searching of today's young Catholics. More generally among these ten recommendations, Hoge and his colleagues recommend the positive promotion of a distinct Catholic identity with an emphasis on sacramental celebration (especially the Eucharist), on the centrality of community and the common good, and the struggle for peace and justice (building on distinctive elements of the strong Catholic tradition in this area).

The recommendation concerning promotion of concern for justice and peace is consistent with the interesting finding that contemporary Catholics view concern for the poor to be an important element of being Catholic. D'Antonio's 2013 study found that 67 percent of Catholics consider helping the poor to be "personally important,"[33] while 88 percent considered concern for the poor to be "personally meaningful" to them.[34] There is no doubt from the teaching and witness of Jesus that concern for the marginalized is a central moral imperative for Christians, and the Catholic Church can be justly proud of its long history of institutional outreach to the disadvantaged and its clear and consistent modern social teaching. It may be that the continuing sense among Catholics that concern for the poor remains central might prove to be an effective meeting point to draw Catholics into a more active contact and participation in the life of the church. Perhaps there is a strategy that leads from shared action on behalf of the poor, through the distinctive Catholic heritage of social concern for the marginalized, within the church's communal life and liturgy, and finally to a deeper encounter with the church's tradition on personal and interpersonal morality.

The importance of strengthening Catholic identity/commitment as well as recommendations like those mentioned above mesh well with the contemporary challenge of the "New Evangelization." The US Catholic Bishops define this challenge in this way:

> The New Evangelization is a call to each person to deepen his or her own faith, have confidence in the Gospel, and possess a willingness to share the Gospel. It is a personal encounter with the person of Jesus, which brings peace and joy. The New Evangelization

---

33. D'Antonio et al., *American Catholics in Transition*, 49.

34. Ibid., 53. At the same time, it must be noted that 60 percent of Catholics say that one can be a "good Catholic" without helping the poor (as opposed to only 44 percent in 1987). Ibid., 50.

provides the lens through which people experience the Church and world around them.[35]

Important methodologies identified by the bishops for promoting a culture of witness and evangelization coincide with those noted above: promotion of parish community life, improving the quality of the parish's liturgical life, supporting family life, and attending to renewed religious education.[36] Promotion of Catholic identity and commitment—with the promotion of the church's moral teaching—go hand-in-hand with the tasks of the New Evangelization.

Catholic Identity and the Life of Virtue

One of the most significant contemporary developments in Christian ethics is the emergence of so-called "virtue ethics."[37] Without denying the role of objective moral norms, many contemporary Catholic moral theologians have begun to focus significantly more attention on virtues—that is, in Thomistic terms, on the "habitual dispositions" that guide and shape our moral decision-making. The emphasis, therefore, is less on rules and more on developing the abiding moral habits—like prudence, justice, temperance, and fortitude—that will enable us to see and to act rightly in moments of choice. The basic moral challenge is not promoting or ensuring adherence to rules but rather forming the virtues that characterize authentic human and Christian living, relating, and acting. At a practical level, given the increasing lack of acceptance of objective moral rules even among Catholics, it may be that the emphasis on the formation of virtues may prove a more immediately fruitful avenue of promoting adult moral formation. In other words, in our culture, we may be able to arrive more easily at a consensus about the attitudes and dispositions that should mark authentic human and Christian living than about rules to be accepted and followed.

To suggest the value of promoting a virtue ethics is not at all to deny the importance of teaching objective moral norms, especially as offered by the magisterium. The complexity of some contemporary moral issues,

---

35. USCCB, *Disciples Called to Witness*, 3.

36. Ibid., 11–14. See also USCCB, *Go and Make Disciples*, 49–79.

37. For a general introduction to virtue ethics, see: Joseph J. Kotva, Jr., *The Christian Case for Virtue Ethics*. For a recent introduction to fundamental moral theology from a virtue-ethics perspective, see William C. Mattison, III, *Introducing Moral Theology: True Happiness and the Virtues*.

especially in medical ethics, cannot be resolved without attention to the norms to guide our decision-making. But formation in virtue and the teaching of moral norms are not mutually exclusive. Both are essential, and both are grounded in a prior strengthening in Catholic identity. In fact, the promotion of virtues would most likely serve the understanding and acceptance of moral norms. Moreover, it is doubtlessly an even more daunting task to try to change the fundamentally subjectivist view of reality that marks our culture than it would be to gain lived adherence to fundamental Christian values, attitudes, and priorities.

The immediate question of a virtue ethics is not "what shall I do?" but "what shall I become?" What kind of person should I be? What kind of person do I want to become? It is precisely from such a fundamental identity that one's action will flow. People's decisions and actions, for good and ill, will flow from the self-identity that they have formed and their vision of the kind of people that they want to be.

The Christian answer to the question of the kind of person that one should become is found in Jesus Christ. Christian faith reveals him as the model of what an authentic person is. It is true that the Gospels contain some particular moral teaching, but its moral teaching focuses more on the kind of attitudes that disciples should foster and the kind of people they should be. Even more basically, the focus of the Gospels is on the person of Jesus who is not only Savior and Lord but also model, teacher, and guide.[38] Likewise, St. Paul addresses moral problems in particular Christian communities of his time, and he sometimes offers concrete moral instruction. But, again, Paul's moral focus is more centrally on the kinds of attitudes and priorities that are appropriate to those who have become one with Christ in baptism.[39]

But Jesus is encountered—and knowledge about and faith in Christ are fostered—within the Christian community. It is important not just to learn about Jesus (conceptual knowledge, facts about Jesus), but to come actually to know him and to enter into relationship with him through prayer, meditation on the Scriptures, the celebration of the sacraments, and the witness of saints. The fundamental vision of the kinds of people that we ought to be and the proper attitudes and priorities that should mark the life of an authentic disciple are not so much taught as witnessed, encountered, imagined, absorbed, embraced, and manifested in action. Like O'Connell,

38. See Harrington and Kennan, *Jesus and Virtue Ethics*.
39. See Harrington and Keenan, *Paul and Virtue Ethics*.

many contemporary virtue ethicists focus on the centrality of community and narrative as the context from which moral self-identity, virtues, and behaviors are transmitted and formed.[40]

Again, we see the central importance and challenge of fostering an inviting community life and vibrant liturgical celebrations to form not just a vague identity of "being Catholic" as one part of one's self-concept but a true and full Christian identity—a committed, participative identity as a disciple of Jesus Christ. Right moral action, which is more than mere adherence to external moral teaching, flows from such an identity and its accompanying virtues. In a time when adherence to the church's moral teaching is linked to active participation—but in a time also when growing numbers of even church-going Catholics view themselves as the final arbiters of moral value—it may be that the emphases of virtue ethics offers an essential element for the moral formation of adult Catholics.

A Broader Vision of Adult Moral Formation

The decline of Catholic identity and commitment, as well as the emergence of contemporary virtue ethics, challenge us to view the work of adult moral formation more broadly. We cannot restrict our view of moral formation to be only the transmission of objective moral rules. Good moral formation is not simply the clearer and more insistent reiteration of the church's moral teaching. No doubt, the church's objective moral teaching on particular issues is valid and essential. Authentic religious education at every level must include such teaching in a way that is accessible and clear. But research study after research study tells us that clarity and regularity of reiteration of teaching is not enough. In fact, alone, it is simply not working. We know that adherence to moral teaching rises with greater participation in the liturgical and communal life of the church, but mere adherence cannot be the true and ultimate goal of Catholic moral teaching. Simply to adhere to an external demand without understanding it or really grasping its truth is the morality of children. Boys and girls obey the rules imposed on them

---

40. The contemporary locating of virtue formation within community is associated especially with the highly influential work of philosopher Alasdair MacIntyre. See: *After Virtue: A Study in Moral Theory*. More specifically in Christian ethics, highly influential is the work of Stanley Hauerwas. See, for example, his early work, *A Community of Character: Toward a Constructive Christian Social Ethic*. For a contemporary Catholic example of this emphasis on community, narrative, and virtues see Paul J. Waddel, *Happiness and the Christian Moral Life*.

either because they fear punishment or want to be considered to be good boys and girls by their parents and significant adults. The fear of hell simply no longer motivates Catholics to accept and live by the church's teaching. (In fact, only about 60 percent of contemporary American Catholics even believe in hell.[41]) As we have seen, attention to the moral authority of the church is declining among American Catholics. No one in a culture of subjectivism (be they pope or mere passerby) could, in any case, legitimately criticize or judge our sincere beliefs or actions as worthy of hell unless those actions clearly harm others.

Contemporary Catholic adults are increasingly non-adherent. Both social scientific study and the emergence of the emphasis on virtue tell us that an effective response to this reality must focus on the promotion of a Christian community life that invites participation, the celebration of the Eucharist and preaching that speaks to Catholics today, the effective offering of the spiritual riches of the Catholic tradition that addresses the spiritual hungers of contemporary men and women, and the call to come together in service of those on the margins of society. It is precisely such priorities that can promote the authentic moral formation of increasingly committed Christians today.

Adult moral formation in our culture must be so much more than merely clear moral catechesis. Its primary focus must be the effort to promote identity, commitment, and participation—not for the sake of mere "adherence" but for the fostering of those Christian attitudes and priorities that lead to right action. It is the encounter with Jesus Christ in the community of the church, centered on the liturgy, celebrating the lives of the saints, and growing in a life of prayerful relationship with Christ that will form Christians in those ways of being that are consistent with the teaching of Christ and of the church.

The foundation of the Christian message is Good News—the Good News that Almighty God in Jesus Christ loves sinners and invites them into relationship and communion. Jesus Christ is the answer to the spiritual yearning of every person in every age and culture. The Christian life is fundamentally, then, a life of response. It is a life of gratitude. To recognize and embrace, in the faith, this Good News demands a grateful response. This is the thankful response of worship, personal and communal, most especially in the celebration of the Eucharist by the community of believers. It is, at the same time, the grateful response of a life that seeks to answer the

---

41. Pew Forum, 2008 U.S. Religious Landscape Survey, 11.

questions: How shall I live in response to this Good News? What kind of person must I become? What shall I do? How shall I act? What kind of relationships shall I foster? To whom will I be loyal? These are the fundamental questions of the Christian moral life, and they are questions that lead to the formation of right attitudes and lead as well to the search for, openness to, and embracing of those moral rules that will serve as reliable guideposts along the way.

The church's moral teaching is for adult Christians who freely embrace it because it makes sense of how they ought to live and the kind of people they want to be. It can be neither imposed nor merely adhered to. The principal task of adult moral formation today, then, is evangelization—reclaiming the Good News of our faith, revitalizing the communal life of the Christian community, announcing God's Word passionately as the answer that it is to life's questions, and celebrating the Eucharist with a lively faith and a welcoming invitation. It is in this context that Christians can truly be formed to live as adult disciples of Jesus. It is here, too, that the church can hope to transmit its moral wisdom to those who wholeheartedly embrace and live the centrality of "being Catholic" in their understanding of themselves in the world of today.

Conclusion

Catholic moral teaching in the United States is in trouble. In the end, pastors and other parish ministers, religious educators, and committed Catholic parents do not need research to tell them this basic fact. But, at the very same time, even while Mass attendance wanes and adherence to moral teaching weakens, we know from experience that the faith is very much alive in parishes, in communities and groups, and in Catholic families. The fundamental tasks of evangelizing and passing on that faith and the way of living that it demands—which are the challenges for Christians in every age and culture—take on their own distinctive shape in our country in our own time. We have seen that, in light of recent research, there is a convergence of proposals and strategies concerning the most effective way to promote Christian moral formation for today. Catholic moral teaching in our country may be in trouble, but most fundamentally the faith is not. It is our challenge to embrace new strategies—and perhaps even new ways of conceiving the task of moral formation—so that the work of evangelizing can bear fruit in our own time.

Bibliography

Center for Applied Research in the Apostolate (CARA). *Sacraments Today: Belief and Practice Among U.S. Catholics.* Washington, DC: CARA, 2008.

D'Antonio, William V., et al. *American Catholics in Transition.* Lanham, MD: Rowman and Littlefield, 2013.

Newport, Frank. "Catholics Similar to Mainstream on Abortion, Stem Cells." Gallup, March 30, 2009. http://www.gallup.com/poll/117154/Catholics-SimilarMainstream-Abortion-Stem-Cells.aspx.

Harrington, Daniel J., SJ, and James F. Keenan, SJ. *Jesus and Virtue Ethics: Building Bridges Between New Testament Studies and Moral Theology.* Lanham, MD: Rowman and Littlefield, 2002.

Harrington, Daniel J., SJ, and James F. Keenan, SJ. *Paul and Virtue Ethics: Building Bridges Between New Testament Studies and Moral Theology.* Lanham, MD: Rowman and Littlefield, 2010.

Hauerwas, Stanley. *A Community of Character: Toward a Constructive Christian Social Ethic.* Notre Dame, IN: University of Notre Dame Press, 1981.

Hoge, Dean R. et al. *Young Adult Catholics: Religion in the Culture of Choice.* Notre Dame, IN: University of Notre Dame Press, 2001.

Kotva, Joseph J., Jr. *The Christian Case for Virtue Ethics.* Washington, DC: Georgetown University Press, 1996.

MacIntyre, Alasdair. *After Virtue: A Study in Moral Theory.* 2nd. ed. Notre Dame, IN: University of Notre Dame Press, 1984.

Mattison, William C., III. *Introducing Moral Theology: True Happiness and the Virtues.* Grand Rapids, MI: Brazos, 2008.

O'Connell, Timothy E. *Making Disciples: A Handbook of Christian Moral Formation.* New York: Crossroad, 1998.

Pew Forum on Religion and Public Life. 2008 U.S. Religious Landscape Survey: Summary of Key Findings. http://religions.pewforum.org/pdf/report2religious-landscape-study-key-findings.pdf.

United States Conference of Catholic Bishops (USCCB), Committee on Evangelization and Catechesis. *Disciples Called to Witness: The New Evangelization.* Washington, DC: USCCB, 2012.

United States Conference of Catholic Bishops (USCCB). *Go and Make Disciples: A National Plan and Strategy for Catholic Evangelization in the United States.* Tenth Anniversary ed. Washington, DC: USCCB, 2002.

Waddel, Paul J. *Happiness and the Christian Moral Life.* 2nd ed. Lanham, MD: Rowman and Littlefield, 2012.

7

Religious Education that Promotes Catholic Identity
A Review and Assessment of Approaches

—Michael P. Horan

Introduction

THIS CHAPTER DESCRIBES THREE approaches to Catholic religious education used widely in parishes in the United States during the last fifty years, and it analyzes these approaches for their implicit but effective contribution to forming Catholic identity. The chapter begins with a descriptive overview of three approaches to religious education in question: (1) a liturgically integrated approach, (2) a shared praxis approach, and (3) a whole community approach. While there are porous boundaries between and among these approaches, each offers a unique angle on religious education/faith formation and furnishes a perspective on the participants, central focus, and activities related to this approach. While each is distinct, the approaches share a common goal: fostering mature faith in Catholic individuals and communities. After considering the general background and select features of each approach to religious education, I argue that each approach, while promoting mature faith, implicitly places an accent on a facet of Catholic identity. Specifically I examine the coherence between these three religious education approaches and three characteristic features of Catholicism, as enunciated by theologian Langdon Gilkey shortly after Vatican Council II.

Gilkey was adept at describing Catholicism in theological terms, contributing an appreciative but analytical voice about Catholicism at the time of the close of Vatican II.[1] Gilkey's framework first suggested characteristic features of Catholicism and supplied a resource for considering "identity" as the Catholic Church confronted modernity fifty years ago. Other theologians, among them Richard McBrien, followed Gilkey's lead.[2] I ask whether and how these characteristic features of Catholicism have been implicitly promoted through the three religious education approaches. The chapter concludes by discussing the potential contributions that religious education leaders can make to the growing concern to foster Catholic identity today.

Context: Religious Education as a Point of Catholic Concern

There is little doubt that religious education, along with liturgy, counts as one of the most visible and measurable features of change in Catholic parish life since the Second Vatican Council.[3] Thomas Walters, quoted by Peter Steinfels in *A People Adrift*, notes that religious education has become a focal point of concern for Catholics leaders, and he contextualizes the concern within a larger pattern of change: the passing away of an integrated Catholic life, in which home, parish, school, neighborhood, and general social norms worked together harmoniously to form Catholics.[4] Here Walters conjures for us a world that once fostered a seamless Catholic identity that Catholics knew, appreciated, and eventually reproduced for their children and grandchildren.[5] Walters suggests that people today confuse two basic but distinct expressions of religious education, schooling and initiation. Confusing schooling, on one hand, with the more general yet influential initiation achieved through family and Catholic social networks on the other, only intensifies the complaints and debates about current Catholic religious education programs and their effectiveness. Walters notes that the confusion of schooling with initiation sometimes causes Catholic educators and church leaders to take sides, emphasizing one expression over the other as the cure for religious education's ills. Walters laments the confusion of schooling and initiation as a wrong diagnosis, and he sees the desire

1. Gilkey, *Catholicism Confronts Modernity*, 113–25.
2. McBrien, *Catholicism*, 2–22.
3. Faggioli, *Vatican II*, 3–4.
4. Steinfels, *A People Adrift*, 233.
5. Ibid., 232.

to pit these approaches against each other as an ineffective cure for religious education in postmodern Catholic America.

Considering the issue of Catholic identity more generally, Steinfels observes that Catholics of the generations that Walters describes formed their self-image, in part, as a victimized and adversarial defense against the Protestant establishment of the nation. This wave of Catholics only came of age a little more than fifty years ago, with the election of John F. Kennedy as president.[6] The election of a Catholic as the nation's president once was regarded as the centerpiece of a narrative about the move from the margins to the mainstream and all the educational, economic, and social success it entailed. David O'Brien,[7] David Gibson,[8] and Gary Wills[9] are among those who offered versions of this narrative.

The move from margins to center, from the self-image of Catholics as outcasts to their place as major players, contributed as well to the formation of a strong Catholic identity, since there existed in that narrative a clear line of distinction between "them" (Protestants) and "us" (Roman Catholics). As Hennesey argued, the growth of Catholics in their *American* identity through social advancement and financial prosperity, and growth in their *Christian* identity in a post-conciliar, ecumenical era, may have diverted their attention from the overarching concern to distinguish Catholics from Protestants.[10]

So is religious education the cause for the loss (or decrease) of a strong Catholic identity? In what follows let us consider three basic religious education approaches that are commonly practiced in Catholic parish life, and ask whether these approaches can implicitly communicate core features of Catholic identity. To do this, let us turn first to a description and analysis of the three approaches.

A Liturgically Integrated Approach

A liturgically integrated approach to religious education is based in the documents, fundamental insights, trajectory, and language of Vatican Council II. Retrieving the language of "catechesis" and reigniting an interest

6. Ibid., 73–74.
7. O'Brien, *The Renewal of American Catholicism*.
8. Gibson, *The Coming Catholic Church*.
9. Wills, *Bare Ruined Choirs*.
10. Hennesey, *American Catholics*.

in the ancient catechumenate, the Second Vatican Council functioned as the impetus for what came to be regarded as a significant shift in religious education theory and practices. The centerpiece of this shift could be seen in the renewed catechumenate, promulgated after the council as the Order of Christian Initiation of Adults. After decades of experience, the Vatican officially acknowledged the restored version of the ancient catechumenate as a successful catechetical effort. Published in 1997, the *General Directory for Catechesis* continues to be the Vatican's official guide to the nature and goals of catechesis. The authors of the document reflect on developments since the Second Vatican Council and assert that "elements of the baptismal catechumenate are now considered as the source of inspiration for all catechesis."[11] It is important to note that the catechumenate was restored and introduced into parish life as a result of the council, but this occurred within a larger agenda concerning the goal of catechesis. According to Richard Reichert, the Council (and the documents that proceeded from it) initiated a shift "toward understanding the goal of catechesis as one of forming disciples of Jesus who would be both willing and capable of participating in a community committed to proclaiming and promoting the reign of God in today's society."[12]

In its documents, principally *Christus Dominus* (Decree Concerning the Pastoral Office of Bishops), the leaders at Vatican II describe the bishop's role in catechesis. In doing so, they adopt the language of catechesis in order to return to the sources of ancient practices, including a concentration on adults and their initiation into the community. The term *catechesis* refers to proclamation, an activity that was likened by the ancients to the work of the poet, who stands on the edge of the stage and speaks a word that rouses the audience's hearts.[13] The related word is *catechumenate*, referring to the ancient process of initiation. While the terms *catechesis* and *catechumenate* initially sounded new and even strange to most American Catholics, the fundamental insights of the ancient catechumenate made their way into parish life through the rituals connected to the renewed version of it, the Rite of Christian Initiation of Adults (RCIA). Various parishes and dioceses in the United States adopted (and sometimes adapted) the RCIA in the two decades following Vatican II. In 1988, the Bishops of the United States mandated its use for adult initiation in parishes.

---

11. Congregation for the Clergy, *General Directory for Catechesis* (GDC), 91.
12. Reichert, *Renewing Catechetical Ministries*, 3.
13. Congregation for the Clergy, GDC, 82.

The RCIA, as the contemporary catechumenate has come to be known widely, contains many liturgical moments that educate both the catechumens and the broader parish, through public rites during the season of Lent. Key rites include the inquiry and welcome of newcomers, the rite of election, and the rite of exorcism. A repeated practice is the dismissal of catechumens from the congregation before the start of the Liturgy of the Eucharist (this practice continues until the high point of the Easter vigil). On Holy Saturday, the assembly both extends and witnesses the ritual welcome of catechumens into the paschal mystery through immersion in the waters of baptism, anointing, and eucharistic sharing. The public nature of these important moments focuses attention on those who are joining the community, but the ritual forms everyone. The rhythm of these rites is a *parish* rhythm, and the parish community would have trouble missing or ignoring these and the other rites that lead up to public moments. Fully initiated members of the parish serve as the witnesses to the process of initiation, watching the catechumens gradually enter into the community through rites during Lent.

The witnessing parishioners constitute more than an audience. They are also supporting actors in this drama, and their faith and ministry skills are formed and honed by the roles they assume as hosts, sponsors, catechists and companions, and ministers of hospitality. Although individuals take up these various roles, the assembly as a whole also has a collective role to play in these scenes. The community must be a welcoming entity, because unless the newcomers and curious inquirers feel welcome into a community, there is no effective or enduring catechumenate, none worthy of the name.

The catechumenate functions as "an inspiration for all catechesis," the authors of the *General Directory for Catechesis* assert.[14] Other processes and programs in parish life have taken their lead from the catechumenate, with activities that are liturgically integrated. They also are based in Scripture and are frequently led or facilitated by lay people. Examples include Bible study circles, series during Advent and Lent, the formal blessing of catechists on Catechetical Sunday each autumn, charismatic renewal groups, the rituals of many lay apostolic movements, and rituals of sending parishioners forth on missions, youth retreats, and community service projects. Some or all of these rituals can be readily found in many parishes. All of them are built on the assumption that Scripture is central to the formation

---

14. Congregation for the Clergy, GDC, 91.

of the community, and that the people are part of an ongoing process of growth in communal prayer.

In addition to its strong ritual elements and its focus on the Word of God, the liturgically integrated approach underscores the freedom of each adult to *decide* and to *commit* to Christian faith and Catholic community in the first place. Notions of decision and commitment align with the shift noted above by Reichert, that formation in discipleship presumes an adult decision in faith and freedom. Because adults are reflecting on their particular experience, the primary metaphor of the faith "journey" seems much more important to them, as the knowledge and experience from which adults can draw is long-standing, varied, and rich. Like a journey, the route can be complicated and interrupted by life's circumstances or an individual's choices. The controlling metaphor of the journey helps to set up the logic of the RCIA as a process. "Journey" presumes no set formula, timeline, or deadline by which to complete the process of initiation. As a result, a second metaphor, that of paschal mystery, stands at center stage in narrating the meaning and measure of the person's journey.[15] Individual catechumens move from their initial inquiry into a deeper reflection, making sense of their past life journey in light of the story of Christ's paschal mystery. In effect, the catechumenate helps adults to "read" their experience on deeper levels that are symbolically connected to the story of Christ and symbolically linked to the ritual actions, sacraments, and sacramentals of the community. The desired outcome of this liturgically integrated approach is the candidate's full initiation into a community, but there is also focus on building and maintaining a community that practices continual and consistent hospitality. In the liturgically integrated approach, the ritual actions of small groups symbolize and affirm the journeys of individuals, each action unique in its details yet sharing a common pattern that is fundamentally relational in character and communally supported.

The liturgically integrated approach to religious education has the advantages of being officially supported by Vatican documents. It also is well established by the US bishops through their endorsement of the RCIA. The approach presumes, but also promotes, an attentive and active Sunday assembly, and it encourages the development of skills within the parish for internal ministries of hospitality and catechesis. In addition, it builds upon the long-standing feature of Catholicism that esteems ritual. Thus it helps to form the "sacramental" identity of Catholics through its many public

---

15. Congregation for the Clergy, GDC, 81.

actions. The liturgically integrated approach promotes a great respect for the sacraments of initiation, encouraging adults to view these sacraments as their entrance into the paschal mystery of Christ's dying and rising, and their welcome into a community that respects and embraces the power of symbols and symbolic action.

A Shared Praxis Approach

The second approach, a shared praxis approach, claims its ancient roots in the *Nicomachean Ethics* of Aristotle, who distinguished among three modes of engaging intelligently in the world: *theoria, praxis,* and *poesis*.[16] *Praxis*, or reflective action, is based in a citizen's free exercise of action in society; an action becomes ethical action, or right living, whenever it is *reflective* action involving twin moments of action and reflection. Contemporary forms of the shared praxis approach can be found in educational theories developed in the second half of the twentieth century, which have affected religious education theory and its practice in the United States in the last forty years.

A well-known theorist of praxis education in the United States was Paolo Freire. Born and educated in Brazil, Freire became Brazil's Minister of Education at a time when the country suffered a staggering rate of illiteracy. He designed situations for education of small groups in conversation, beginning with pictures and moving to text, so that people could read critically and come to a hopeful but informed awareness, a consciousness that he termed "conscientization." For Freire, the underlying issue for his people was liberation from poverty, with illiteracy being a symptom of the pressing need for measurable social change. He asserted that reading can lead to liberation. Freire, who later left Brazil and taught at Harvard, made his theory of general education for conscientization well-known to educators in the United States.[17] Freire proffered that by analyzing the situation that words encode, people become literate in two senses. First, readers are able to step back and reflect on the situation, the action that makes the text (whether pictures or prose) possible. Second, this kind of reflection allows people to step back and to ask why, to notice, name, and critique the injustices of present situations and thus to be conscientized, awakened afresh to injustice and its causes, and thereby empowered to act.

---

16. Aristotle, *Nicomachean Ethics*, book 7, chapter 7.
17. Freire, *Education for Critical Consciousness*.

A shared praxis approach in *religious* education is a hallmark of the work of Thomas Groome, professor of theology and religious education at Boston College. Through his extensive writing, teaching, public presentations, and workshops in the United States and abroad, Groome has helped to give language and form to an approach to faith formation that promotes the essential gospel message of justice through religious education, and which is related to, though distinct from, Freire's model. Groome's shared praxis approach inculcates a focus on the Christian life as *praxis*, as *doing* the gospel and reflecting on the action of sharing faith. The shared praxis approach rests on the assumption that people can actually hear and appropriate the Word of God when that Word becomes effective in their lives. The Christian gospel, what Groome terms the "Story and Vision," is most alive and effective when it is in conversation with the story of people's individual life of faith and communal life. In his programmatic theoretical writing for religious education leaders, and through his translation of these ideas into texts for children and their parents, Groome enunciates a process that seeks to foster people's transformation *within* them, even as it narrates that transformative power *to* them.[18] Groome refers to these moments of transformation as "movements" within the process of shared praxis, designed to engage people in reflection on action. The movements help participants, first, to name their "story" or present action; second, to encounter (or re-encounter) the "vision" of Christ and the Christian commitment to the reign of God; third, to consider the relationships between the individual's story and the larger story and vision of the community (whether these are compatible or dialectic relationships); finally, to commit to renewed action that will inculcate the values of the reign of God in one's life and in the world.[19] Persons of any age can participate in these "movements" of shared praxis. In fact, the experience of sharing faith can be intergenerational, not confined to particular or discrete age groups or interest cohorts within a large or a small community. Groome's texts for children are aimed at translating his process for both children and their parents, so that parents can become acquainted (or re-acquainted) with the story and vision of Christianity in conversation with their own story, before and while they attempt to form their children in Christian faith.

The desired outcome for the group engaged in shared praxis is a commitment to the reign of God. The outcome may rightly be regarded as more

---

18. Groome, *Christian Religious Education*.
19. Ibid., 4–15.

expansive than the outcome associated with the liturgically integrated approach. A liturgically integrated approach to religious education attends to the internal life of the parish community first and foremost, welcoming catechumens into an existing community. By contrast, the shared praxis approach, like the educational theory of Freire, seeks to propel its participants toward the world through a critical reading of their own life situation in all its dimensions, an encounter with the vision of Jesus, and a commitment to justice and action on behalf of the reign of God in the world. Parish activities and programs such as *Just Faith* and *Pax Christi USA* furnish concrete examples of shared praxis; they combine service with Catholic social teaching and social analysis. These are explicit examples of ways that individuals and communities can reflect on the central message of the gospel of justice and on the relationship between the Christian Story and their individual and collective stories. Shared praxis as a method can be integrated into many processes within a parish, so that people become attuned to consider and assess individual or communal actions against the measure of their commitment to the reign of God. Whenever people take stock of situations in conversation with the larger "Story and Vision" of the gospel, they are confronting the cost of being Jesus's disciples.[20] The approach has the advantage of fostering the church's engagement with the wider world rather than merely with the welfare of its internal members, thus attracting the attention of Catholics and non-Catholics alike. Shared praxis provides faith formation opportunities for people to connect and integrate spirituality and action, and to understand the potential of the Catholic faith to effect change in society.

A Whole Community Approach

The third approach to religious education, as its name suggests, draws in the entire parish community, and it presumes everyone participates in the work of religious education. Its participants are identified as the whole community, and the whole life of that community functions as the "curriculum" from which people of all ages learn. The whole community approach shares much with the liturgically integrated approach described above, placing high value on the rituals that shape a community. It differs from the liturgically integrated approach in that it focuses neither on the initiation of newcomers nor on liturgy. Rather, it attends to all aspects of parish

20. Ibid., 12–15.

life as its curriculum. Like the shared praxis approach, the whole community approach can draw people of different ages and life stages together for reflection, but the whole community approach identifies all the church's activities as formative. It seeks to enunciate the content for religious education as very expansive and multi-faceted, including but not limited to either liturgy or justice-making. It presumes that all the parishioners can function as catechists—agents of religious education. Evidence of interest in this approach can be seen as early as the 1930s in Europe, and, as Huebsch notes, it has become popular in many parishes in the United States.[21]

A whole community approach can be found in movements in religious education reaching back to the early part of the twentieth century. For example, in his classic work, *The Good News and Our Proclamation of the Faith*, first published in 1936 as *Die Frohbotshaft und Unserer Glaubensverkundigung*, Josef Jungmann asserted that the content of Catholic religious education should achieve an integration of liturgy, Bible, Christian service or good works, and doctrine.[22] According to Jungmann's vision, all these elements constitute the content of religious education. While focusing principally on children's religious education and only tangentially on the catechumenate, Jungmann hoped that Bible and liturgy might be integrated into children's lessons so that the learners would be moved to understand and appreciate the unitary nature of the good news. He argued that understanding the whole of Christian faith would motivate the learners to works of charity and service out of gratitude rather than obligation.[23] Lamenting the fragmentation of the Christian message of salvation into component parts, Jungmann regarded the content of religious education more expansively than his peers, but his focus remained principally on teaching children and youth.

Jungmann promoted a wider notion of the *content* of religious education. A more expansive notion of the *participants* in religious education would be the contribution of the next generation of scholars. Such was the case for Maria Harris, who built on the foundational work of Jungmann. In *Fashion Me a People*, Harris taught that the daily living of Christian faith by community members is the "curriculum" to be mined and studied by every adult parishioner. Harris outlined the five major facets of a community's life as *leiturgia* (liturgy), *didache* (teaching), *diaconia* (service and justice),

---

21. Huebsch, *Whole Community Catechesis*.
22. Jungmann, *The Good News and Our Proclamation*, 4–11.
23. Jungmann, *The Good News*, 75–76.

kerygma (proclamation and preaching), and *koinonia* (community). Harris proposed that the whole community can be involved in each of these facets, and that Christians apprehend the whole Christian message most deeply by living it. Thus, disciples come to understand the curriculum of the church's life in simultaneous, dual roles: as both participants in, and as observers of, the way a faith community conducts itself.[24] For Harris, the local community, congregation, or parish does not need a curriculum external to itself to account for itself. The church *is* the curriculum, in all the aspects of its life that make it an authentic expression of the gospel. It teaches by living, and it lives a healthy existence when the community is aware that it is forming everyone more deeply in their identity, and it is doing this all the time.

Often this approach both intrigues and challenges parish leaders and their imaginations, as the approach can seem large, far-reaching, holistic, and perhaps even amorphous. Hence it has at times been tamed, domesticated into discrete programs for age cohorts, or family sessions that allow parents and children to come together after a session with their peers. But the original vision associated with this approach is grand. The approach finds expression in select liturgies, parish retreats or events that are parish-wide, with good potential to include persons who are not part of a traditional two-generation household, and to help participants catch themselves as they assume roles of teacher and learner. Virtual participation through the Internet also extends participation to those who might not be able or willing to join a physical gathering space, but who want some connection to the community. If the life of the church supplies the curricular content, then this approach requires that community leaders and parishioners, particularly adult parishioners, be both willing participants and participant observers in the formation of the church. When they do this, the community can flourish, and individuals can find a place in one or another of the many facets of the curriculum. Through this whole community approach, as John Roberto and other faith formation leaders have argued, the church becomes a communion of lifelong learners. Just as important, the church's adult members begin to understand this approach by attending to their own behaviors.[25] By being attentive, adults can recognize, esteem, and harness the potential of each occasion to be a formative moment for themselves and others, a moment that knits together teaching and learning faith. In

---

24. Harris, *Fashion Me a People*, 63.
25. Roberto, *Becoming a Church*, 11–20.

Harris's vision of a whole community, as adults are being formed, they also are forming successive generations, and children are forming their elders.

Do These Approaches Foster Catholic Identity?

We have briefly considered three approaches to religious education that leaders in the field can readily recognize in various forms of parish life in the United States today. The liturgically integrated approach reaches its most easily recognized parish expression in the catechumenate or RCIA. While originally focused on adult participants, principles of the catechumenate have been adapted to groups of various ages. When the RCIA is most vibrant, the parish community functions as a collective sponsor to the catechumens. When principles of the catechumenate are translated for other learners and other situations, the outcome of the liturgically integrated approach is a vibrant worshipping community where fully vested parishioners respond by ministering to the newcomers and to one another, based in the Word of God.

The shared praxis approach rests on a commitment to reflective action, to do the gospel and to reflect on it in a variety of settings, groups, and situations. Participants in the shared praxis approach can be persons of any age or stage of life, but the common outcome is a deeper commitment to the reign of God, typically manifested in reflective action on behalf of justice. The approach is helpful to small groups as well as large ones, serving to issue and clarify the challenging message of the gospel. As an approach it promotes conscientization of a kind that can galvanize a community toward service or justice actions as visible, measurable, and powerful outcomes. It has the potential to evangelize outsiders by gaining the attention of persons who are currently not active in parish life and who do not attend parish events.

The third approach, focused on the whole community, presumes a rich and multifaceted content for religious education, as noted by Jungmann, and it highly values the community and all aspects of the community, summarized in the five facets of the church's "curriculum" distilled by Harris. Promoters of this approach imagine that the participants include everyone, all the time, and the outcome of this approach is for everyone to notice, identify, learn, and appreciate the many ways the faith curriculum is taught. Promoters of this approach also highly prize the community as both teachers and learners, with the community's activities and ways of being serving as the content to be communicated. The desired outcome of a whole community approach is a vibrant life of faith supported by a community that embraces the multifaceted Christian message and is eager to share it.

These three approaches to religious education have porous boundaries, but each emphasizes a dimension of Catholic identity by virtue of its method, as well as its sphere of concern for catechetical outcomes. Each implicitly carries forward an aspect of Catholic identity first articulated by Langdon Gilkey and later elaborated on by others. Gilkey, one of the few non-Catholic observers whom the pope invited to Vatican II, was a theologian at the University of Chicago. Upon his return from the council, Gilkey attempted to name the theological differences between Catholic and Protestant Christianity, not in terms of each community's particular practices, but in terms of select theological themes that distinguish one stream of Christian tradition from another. He sparked a discussion that others continued; among them were theologians Richard McBrien[26] and David Tracy,[27] sociologist of religion Andrew Greeley,[28] and religious educator Thomas Groome.[29] Consistent with Gilkey's initial writing, all these authors described Catholic identity through theological themes.

The three theological themes of Catholicism to be distilled from a reading of these authors are *sacramentality*, *mediation*, and *communion*. These themes constitute distinctive features of a Catholic way of being in the world. They are not exclusive to Catholicism, but they are communicated and emphasized in a particular way through Catholic life. The following analysis of these themes is designed to achieve two goals. First, in keeping with the ecumenical intentions of Gilkey and others, I want to note that Catholic emphases differ from Protestant emphases in degree but not in kind; that is, the Catholic Church may be closely associated with a theological theme, but that theme can be found in all Christian communities. Second, to follow the lead of Gilkey and others, I specifically distinguish underlying themes from the general plots that often take center stage in discussions of Catholic identity. For example, it would be true to assert that Catholics honor Mary and the saints through processions and prayers. Catholics wear ashes on Ash Wednesday, hold eucharistic adoration on Holy Thursday night, and venerate the cross on Good Friday. Each of these practices signals a plot, a

---

26. McBrien, *Catholicism*.
27. Tracy, *The Analogical Imagination*.
28. Greeley, *The Catholic Imagination*.
29. Groome, *Sharing Faith*.

specific ritual behavior at a particular moment. Each Catholic practice sets Catholics apart from most other Christians. All of these actions taken together illustrate the underlying theme of sacramentality, in which symbols communicate Catholic truths, often by using earthly things. McBrien asserts that Catholic life is studded with such symbolic actions and informed by a sacramental sensibility: "The Catholic vision sees God in and through all things.... The visible, the tangible, the finite, the historical—all these are actual or potential carriers of the divine presence."[30]

Using the term sacramentality, Gilkey and others reflect on that feature of Catholic life that prizes ritual and connects its ritual to people's imagination about God. Catholic sacramental life is based in what Tracy terms the analogical imagination, in which one imagines that human experience of God is analogous to how God really is.[31] An analogical imagination posits that there is more similarity than difference between humans and God because of the core principle of the Incarnation. The generous use of ritual actions, symbols, sacraments, and sacramental signs—all common to Catholic worship—can be found in the liturgically integrated approach to religious education. The community emphasizes its welcome and its identity through sacramental signs and ritual actions. These signs and actions are essential to the formation of the catechumens, who are immersed in the waters of death and resurrection, anointed with oil as a symbol of the Spirit's strength, and invited to share at the table of the Lord. The eucharistic sharing occurs through sacramental elements of bread and wine that, according to Catholic worship and teaching, reveal much more than mere bread and wine. While the sacraments are touchstones for the life of the community, they also orient the community members to the importance of rituals beyond the sacraments. Catechumens consider the meaning of the rituals through the "mystagogical catecheses" that follow Easter and entrance as full members of the community, and all the people reflect on these rituals through homilies and catechetical sessions.

A liturgically integrated approach rests on the principle of sacramentality and promotes an appreciation for symbolic actions and ritual gestures of the kind found in many religious education programs and processes. These include, but are not limited to, ritual blessings in churches or schools, parents blessing their children as they leave home, small groups that reflect on the lectionary readings for the coming Sunday, lighting of the Advent

---

30. McBrien, *Catholicism*, 10.
31. Tracy, *The Analogical Imagination*.

wreath, dramatic enactments of the Gospels, and retreats that incorporate symbolic actions.

Mediation, our second theological theme, is a corollary to the theme of sacramentality. Symbols and sacraments affirm God's presence in creation, God's power within all that is experienced through human sensory perception in this world. Catholicism has a rich tradition of affirming the mediating power of the ordained priest. But this principle of mediation extends also to the baptized, since God's desire for the world, God's reign, requires ethical actions by humans toward one another and toward creation. Ethical actions matter, because humans matter. As the stewards of creation, humans possess both responsibilities and power. Catholic ethicist Richard Gula notes that power, correctly used, can have an effect on the world in order to foster and extend God's reign.[32] Conversely, power can be abused. Humans do not accomplish anything without God, but humans can either promote or curtail God's reign in the world.

The theme of mediation is present in the shared praxis approach to religious education. The shared praxis approach fosters awareness of the power of human action in the world; it helps its participants to consider their potency and agency to proclaim and promote God's reign. Participants interrogate their own experience to discern whether and how human actions are aligned with the gospel and Jesus's dream for a just world. Participants also consider whether and how human actions frustrate, postpone, or reverse that dream. The shared praxis approach to religious education rests on the assumption of mediation as an enduring value for Catholics. God's power, mediated through the sacramental life, is the source of human creation and invention. God's power, mediated in the world through human cooperation with God's plan and human agency, is the source of right action, social transformation, and ecological healing of the world God created.

Our third theological theme is communion. Communion rests on the bedrock conviction that all experience of God is not only mediated, it is mediated and grounded in some form of community. There is in Catholicism no simple way to sustain a relationship with God without a communal context. The obvious one for most Catholics is the parish community, but there are many other possibilities: religious communities and monasteries, lay societies and apostolic movements, sodalities and third orders. Catholicism's emphasis on the church community or *ecclesia* as a way to God aligns itself readily with the whole community approach to religious education.

32. Gula, *Just Ministry*.

In the whole community approach, every aspect of the church's life carries the potential to form and transform persons of every age, circumstance, and stage of life, all of it occurring in the communal context. The whole community approach esteems and illustrates the communal nature of faith according to the Catholic tradition. When the church is teaching, some part of the church is also watching, listening, and learning.

There are clear counterpoints to these Catholic themes in Protestant practices and the theologies that they convey. As McBrien observes, the Protestant theological tradition "raises a word of caution" about these themes, notes the dangers of expressing them too strongly, and offers a corrective balance to them. Sacramentality, taken to its extreme, becomes empty ritualism or idolatry. Mediation overemphasized, without reference to the divine source of that mediation, devolves into a form of magic. Strong emphasis on communion, without sufficient respect for the individual conscience or human freedom, can lead to collectivism and blind loyalty.[33]

Although there are cautions to be noted and overemphasis to be avoided, the positive potential of these Catholic themes lies in their inclusive nature. They offer a way to describe Catholic identity that contemporary parishioners may find culturally and theologically unifying and ecumenically sensitive. Pastoral leaders may find them pastorally effective for at least three reasons.

First, the church is a culturally pluralistic body, and the many ethnic cultures within it embody the themes of sacramentality in distinct ways. For instance, the ritual movements, processions, and titles used to honor Mary vary from culture to culture. But all the cultures hold a sense of sacramentality in common. Thus, a theme such as sacramentality may offer a way to narrate particular cultural expressions of faith found in each ethnic group, to respect cultural differences, and to find common ground for coherent speech about Catholic identity that transcends particular ethnic cultures and unites them rhetorically and theologically.

Second, the domestic church in the United States is an ecumenical church. The results of the Pew Forum US Religious Landscape Survey show that Catholics are now marrying non-Catholics at unprecedented rates.[34] The themes may help Catholics, and the pastoral ministers who support them, to account for Catholicism in a way that moves beyond what Catholics oppose (abortion, death penalty, gay marriage) and the beliefs or practices that

33. McBrien, *Catholicism*, 13.
34. *U.S. Religious Landscape Survey*.

distinguish Catholics from Protestants (real presence, seven sacraments, papal infallibility). The themes may furnish a different and attractive starting point for ecumenical conversations within the domestic church, moving from the common themes to the particular expression of those themes in the respective Christian churches. The statistics found in the Pew Forum studies tell us that the domestic church is an ecumenical church. The domestic church could be enriched by conversations that probe differences while maintaining the conditions of trust and respect that are essential to effective ecumenical dialogue. The three theological themes may help Christians to engage in such dialogue at home as well as in the public square.

Third, currently the unity of the Catholic Church in the United States is strained by differing theologies and interpretations of its own history and more recent experiences of what it means to be Catholic.[35] The themes of sacramentality, mediation, and communion may not universally satisfy the hunger for a distinctive Catholic identity, but they could help to foster conversations across theological divisions. The themes of sacramentality, mediation, and communion may serve as a common platform to begin such conversations, and thus promote much-needed intra-ecclesial dialogue about what constitutes Catholic identity.

Each of the three approaches to religious education we have considered places an accent on an essential facet of Catholic identity. The liturgically integrated approach showcases the theological theme of sacramentality, with its focus on the catechumenate and the rich symbolism of Catholic ritual that it communicates. The shared praxis approach awakens attention to the Catholic theme of mediation and the potency of human ingenuity, invention, and effort to achieve social justice. Grounded in an Aristotelian understanding of ethical action on behalf of the common good, and consistent with contemporary notions of *praxis*-based education for social change, this approach celebrates the mediating power of the human being (and communities) to cooperate with God's reign of justice. The whole community approach centers upon the importance of the church and the ways in which its life reveals the modes of Christian discipleship, acquired and understood best by living them. Aligned with and expressing the theological theme of communion, this approach to religious education challenges the church to learn from its own inner life and external actions what it means to be a true disciple, and to look to the community as both teacher and learner.

35. Steinfels, *A People Adrift*.

Conclusion

This analysis of three religious education approaches suggests that Catholic parishioners are learning from and teaching each other by methods that inculcate appreciation for key theological themes about Catholic identity. The theological themes of sacramentality, mediation, and communion reside implicitly in the three religious education approaches we have considered. They could be made more explicit by adept leaders within the parish who help others to appreciate these themes, the connections between these themes and religious education, and the potential contribution that effective religious education can make to the larger conversation about Catholic identity. By effectively highlighting how some standard religious education practices communicate essential themes of Catholic identity, pastoral leaders could contribute to that conversation in constructive, non-adversarial ways.

Bibliography

Aristotle. *Nicomachean Ethics*. Translated by H. Rackham. Cambridge: Harvard University Press, 1982.

Congregation for the Clergy. *General Directory for Catechesis* (GDC). Washington, DC: United States Catholic Conference, 1997.

Faggioli, Massimo. *Vatican II: The Battleground for Meaning*. New York: Paulist, 2012.

Freire, Paulo. *Education for Critical Consciousness*. New York: Seabury, 1973.

Gibson, David M. *The Coming Catholic Church: How the Faithful Are Shaping a New American Catholicism*. San Francisco: Harper, 2003.

Gilkey, Langdon B. *Catholicism Confronts Modernity: A Protestant View*. New York: Seabury, 1975.

Greeley, Andrew M. *The Catholic Imagination*. Berkeley: University of California Press, 2000.

Groome, Thomas H. *Christian Religious Education: Sharing Our Story and Vision*. San Francisco: Harper and Row, 1980.

———. *Sharing Faith: A Comprehensive Approach to Religious Education and Pastoral Ministry*. San Francisco: Harper San Francisco, 1991.

Gula, Richard M. *Just Ministry: Professional Ethics for Pastoral Ministers*. New York: Paulist, 2010.

Harris, Maria. *Fashion Me a People: Curriculum in the Church*. Louisville, KY: Westminster John Knox, 1989.

Hennesey, James. *American Catholics: A History of the Roman Catholic Community in the United States*. New York: Oxford University Press, 1981.

Huebsch, Bill. *Whole Community Catechesis in Plain English*. Mystic, CT: Twenty-Third, 2002.

Jungmann, Josef A. *Die Frohbotschaft und Unserer Glaubensverkundigung*. Regensburg: Pustet, 1936.

———. *The Good News Yesterday and Today*. Translated by William A. Huesman. New York: Sadlier, 1962.

———. *Handing on the Faith: A Manual of Catechetics*. New York: Herder and Herder, 1959.

McBrien, Richard P. *Catholicism*. San Francisco: Harper San Francisco, 1994.

O'Brien, David J. *The Renewal of American Catholicism*. New York: Paulist, 1971.

Reichert, Richard. *Renewing Catechetical Ministry: A Future Agenda*. New York: Paulist, 2002.

Roberto, John. *Becoming a Church of Lifelong Learners*. Mystic, CT: Twenty-Third, 2006.

Steinfels, Peter. *A People Adrift: The Crisis of the Roman Catholic Church in America*. New York: Simon & Schuster, 2003.

Tracy, David. *The Analogical Imagination: Christian Theology and the Culture of Pluralism*. New York: Crossroad, 1986.

Wills, Gary. *Bare Ruined Choirs: Doubt, Prophecy, and Radical Religion*. Garden City, NY: Doubleday, 1972.

U.S. Religious Landscape Survey. http://religions.pewforum.org.

www.ingramcontent.com/pod-product-compliance
Lightning Source LLC
Chambersburg PA
CBHW051941160426
43198CB00013B/2248